THE WEALTH

SCORE EXPERT

Discover the Fourth Score Secretly Used

by Banks and Financial Institutions

Table of Contents

PREFACE

I've been in the credit solutions business for about 15 years, and I came across a few challenges when I was trying to expand my credit.

I got up to an 816 credit score. My scores went up and down, but I think the highest I've ever been was 845. I started from a 486 credit score. I had 49 negative notations.

I lived fast and hard. I was born and raised in the ghetto. So every time someone offered me something by way of credit I said, yes!

The only protocol I had was how soon I could get the credit card and start using it? I was not worried about the 35% payment history rule or the 30% amount of use rule. I wasn't concerned about any of the rules of credit. I was only interested in seeing approvals or hearing banks and financial institutions saying yes. Soon after getting tons of credit, I got myself in trouble.

I got about two hundred thousand dollars or more in debt. More like $242,000. I ran into a major setback in my life. I had a beautiful child, a little girl with my college sweetheart. She decided to leave me and go off to pursue another relationship. I took this very hard, as I was from a family where a man and his family were supposed to stay together forever.

My father and my mother got married when my mother was only 16 years of age, and my father died after 43 years of marriage. So I took a hard hit mentally and spiritually when my family left and moved in with another gentleman.

I could not work. I could not eat. I couldn't sleep. I couldn't do anything about her choice, and I eventually lost my way. I did not lose my mind. I just lost my way. So some time had passed I woke up out of my fog and was not able to maintain my lifestyle.

My two cars were repossessed. I was evicted from my house. My nineteen credit cards were in default. My thirteen department store cards were in default. I had visited the emergency room on three separate occasions thinking I had a heart attack. I was essentially having anxiety attacks. I was moving from place to place, room to room and leaving utilities behind that was following me on my credit report because the creditors couldn't figure out where to mail the statements. So eventually I ended up moving to Las Vegas to hide from my shame. I arrived in Las Vegas with around 49 negative notations on my credit reports. So I knew I had to fix my credit.

So after fixing my credit, I realized that I wanted to do more with my credit. I wanted to leave something behind for my daughter. I didn't just want to amass fancy things anymore. I wanted to have a legacy, and I knew that my credit could be used for more than the establishment of debt.

I believed the average individual was not only looking to meet their needs with credit but also looking to have it as a cushion to their income. So when I came to this realization, I decided to leverage my 800 credit scores differently! I wanted to become an investor in real estate.

So, I started looking at my credit differently. I started trying to maximize my credit limits to leverage it and invest to get passive income. Quickly, I hit a wall. I was having challenges acquiring more credit.

I realized that even with an 800 credit scores banks were still giving me relatively low limits. I was wondering how some people have high credit card limits, like fifty thousand, seventy-five thousand, and even one hundred thousand.

So I started doing some research and keeping fact sheets on my clients that had higher limits and the clients that had lower limits.

I found some nuances about credit that most people don't know. I discovered that before FICO was mainstream to the general public to understand, banks and financial institutions told applicants that their credit score was being used to determine their risk factor.

However, lenders did not tell applicants from who, what, or where they got the score from or what the name of the score was? So applicants would walk away from the table confused and be trying to figure out what this mysterious score that's preventing their application approval is?

So eventually this mysterious credit score became a challenge because so many people were being excluded out of the credit industry and out of the financial markets. And since credit makes the world go around contrary to what most of us believe that cash is king when in reality credit is king.

After the growing interest of US citizens and the review of the matter by local officials, FICO decided to reveal their algorithm or the characteristics of their credit scoring model. That's when we got the FICO chart.

So banks were using this black box credit score for so many years to determine loan repayment risk and even if an applicant had a good job, been there more than two years, five years, ten years or whatever, paid their bills on time, this score still had a more significant impact than the actual credit profile in some cases.

So when I discovered this fact, I immediately started keeping a record of the approval amounts our clients would get from our credit rebuilder program. After repairing our client's credit, we would send them all to the same local creditors to apply for new tradelines.

So I sent Brad over to the same bank as his college buddy, Brian. They both graduated from the same university. They both lived in the same house. They both worked at the same company, and they both had been there the same amount of time. Brad and Brian had a similar amount of inquiries as well. So their credit profiles were almost a mirror image. Brad was approved for a $500 credit limit, and Brian got approved for a $1,500 credit limit. I could not figure out why there was a difference between Brian's credit approval and Brad's credit approval? They were the same age, graduated from the same high school and college, living at the same address, and working with the same employer. Why does one have a more upper credit limit than the other?

I'll tell you why. FICO was providing credit scores based on their secret algorithm, and consumer data they collected about you and selling it to the banks and the banks would use it as a determinant of risk in their consideration on extending you a loan.

When the FICO score was found out, the banks didn't stop using proprietary tools to mitigate risk. New tools to evaluate applications and risk were being developed to help all lenders collect and process consumer data. One, in particular, was the creation of consumer files. So there's a difference between a consumer report, a credit report, and a consumer file.

So let's talk about that. A credit report is when you're applying for credit, and you don't even get a copy of it from the bank. If you apply for credit, the mortgage professional will not give you your report, the auto dealer will not give you your report, and the realtor will not give you your report. They'll tell you, oh no we can't give it to you. We can show it to you, but we can't give it to you. Right?

So the credit report doesn't belong to you. They'll tell you to go to the credit bureaus and get it right? So that's a credit report.

Then there's a consumer report. A consumer report is when you want to review your report for yourself and you get it directly from the credit bureau.

But the consumer file is what's most important to banks and lenders because that's what FICO was. It was a consumer file when the general public was not familiar with its use. It was the consumer data that was gathered about you from exclusive places that you didn't know about.

So now I've discovered a list of consumer files use by financial institutions, I was able to figure out why Brad got a $500 approval and Brian got a $1,500 approval. It was the difference in consumer data the banks had on brad and Brian. For example, you ever noticed on a credit app that creditors ask you for your mother's maiden name? Yes. What's your mother have to do with this?

Because if your mother, I'm sorry to say this, but if your mother was poor and you happened to move away from the area that you used to live in, and now you're out in a better environment, banks want to know where you relocated from. Why, not just because you moved, but because knowing your history as an applicant can help bankers trace your family name. So bankers ask about your mother's maiden name.

What they do is check the demographics of where your mother lives by scraping for data in your consumer files, credit reports, affiliated companies and their subsidiaries. Bankers may discover from LexisNexis that your mother lived in a zip code in your hometown LexisNexis had a crime rate of 47%, had an average education of a ninth grader, the average home value in that zip code was less than 30,000.

So now armed with this additional consumer data collected from obscure consumer files bankers have a better chance to mitigate their risk approving loans they may default.

So if lending institutions are using LexisNexis to collect statistical data about the zip code where you currently live, the crime rate in that area, the education level in that zip code, it's not difficult to see how some applicants with similar applications can have factors that cause them to get wildly different approvals.

So for this example, let's say Brad's family name was from the urban part of the city and Brian's family name was from a suburban area. Brad's last address through LexisNexis had a higher crime rate, a lower education rate and a lower average home value in that part of the city. This could potentially explain why Brad's approval was lower than Brains. So with this information, I decided to collect a list of all the consumer files I could find and then write them to request copies of my file.

I'm going to give you a secret I never told anyone else. This is the first time I've spoken in a public forum about this. So how did I find these consumer files?

Well, I've been doing credit repair the old-fashioned way for thirteen years. I'm still requesting our client's consumer reports to review and to dispute from the data therein. After, auditing the reports of Brad and Brian and meticulously going through each page I noticed a section of the reports that most credit experts overlook. It's the promotional inquiries section. We call these soft inquiries.

No one sees them on the credit reports because they are not listed there and because mostly everyone in the credit repair space is doing online disputing no one sees too many consumer reports anymore. Because everything is digital now and being in the millennial age where most typically prefer to conduct credit repair via online systems and software.

I was always looking at disputing some of the hard inquiries but had very little interest in the promotional inquiries. But guess what, this is where you'll find the consumer files and the companies that aggregate and store data about you.

Consumer files like SageStream, Advanced Resolution Solutions, and Innovis before they became credit bureaus.

These companies were consumer files that banks were using privately.

Also, there's a consumer file that is so impactful to you potentially getting approved for big money that is scary. Did you know that the credit bureaus own payroll companies? Yeah. They own payroll companies. So when you apply, you say you make this amount they have a payroll company arm that they buy your real-time paycheck from the last two weeks.

Also, did you know credit bureaus own rental bureaus and can access detailed data about your rental history that's not on your credit reports? Yes!

Did you know that bankers can now pull your banking activities report and see exactly how many deposits, debits, and credits you've had in real time and they consult this information unbeknownst to you. I found the reports.

I will stop here, but I wrote a book called The Wealth Score Expert where I reveal in more detail a list of most of the consumer files banks and lending institutions use. But more importantly, I want to tell you that there is a new score emerging called the wealth score.

It's not just about credit reports anymore. We're in a data-driven age where it's more about granular consumer data, and credit report require too much red tape, too many people involved, too many signatures, too much potential for lawsuits due to database breaches.

Our consumer files are consulted by lenders and they never even tell us in most cases. It's like me going to your Facebook and not telling you I was there, that's how powerful the Wealth Score is becoming.

So I found this secret file that most of the banks were reviewing. I couldn't figure out why I couldn't get approvals for higher limits until I got a copy of this file. This file had a copy of all of my banking history for 36 months, and all of the banks that I was applying with were requesting this when I completed applications for credit.

And because I wasn't keeping any money in this account; it was a credit union account that I would use to get great car loans and stuff with I wasn't keeping much money in the account.

However, that was the account the banks were consulting, not the account where I kept the bulk of my money. So when I found out the banks were using this file, I froze that file. Some of my limits were increased on my credit cards. Guess what I started doing? I decided to freeze all of my consumer files. Safe Rent, ChexSystems, LexisNexis, Innovis, Advanced Resolution Solutions and more. There are many more of these secret files that I review in detail in my book The Wealth Score Expert. I just gave you a snapshot of the book here.

So, if you're trying to get access to more money, you got to go to the granular files, and there's so many out there it's scary. But the ones that I found, a total of seventy-seven of them are the ones that most banks use. I know which bank use which ones too.

I have a website called WealthScores.com Okay. And you can go there to get an overview of some of these consumer files I can freeze and see the services I offer and the investment needed by you and potentially you can get free credit repair with Wealth Score repair.

INTRODUCTION

To score is human. Ranking individuals by grades and other performance numbers are as old as human society. Consumer scores, numbers given to individual's to describe or predict their characteristics, habits, or predilections are a modern day numeric shorthand that ranks separates sifts, and otherwise, categorizes individuals and also predicts their potential future actions.

Consumer scores abound today. Credit scores based on credit files receive much public attention, but many more types of consumer scores exist. They are used widely to predict behaviors like, spending, health, fraud, profitability, and much more. These scores rely on petabytes of information coming from newly available data streams.

The information can be derived from many data sources and can contain financial, demographic, ethnic, racial, health, social, and other data.

The Consumer Profitability Score, Individual Health Risk Score. Summarized Credit Statistics that score a neighborhood for financial risk, fraud scores, and many others seek to predict how consumers will behave based on their past behavior and characteristics.

Predictive scores bring varying benefits and drawbacks. Scores can be correct, or they can be wrong or misleading. Consumers cores – created by either the government or the private sector – threaten privacy, fairness, and due process because scores, particularly opaque scores with unknown ingredients or factors, can too easily evade the rules established to protect consumers. The most salient feature of modern consumer scores is the scores are typically secret in some way. The existence of the score itself, its uses, the underlying factors, data sources, or even the score range may be hidden. Consumer scores with secret factors.

The following information relates to the understanding and use of a credit score. Listed are details regarding the determination of a credit score, how you can find out what your credit score is, and what you can do if you have questions about your credit score. Such information is critical when borrowing finances for personal or business use.

The point of this information sheet is to make you aware of issues related to the secrets surrounding credit scores and how to managing your credit prudently to ensure a good credit score. The Scoring of America sources and secret algorithms can be obnoxious, unaccountable, untrustworthy, and un- auditable. Secret scores can be wrong, but no one may be able to find out that they are wrong or what the truth is.

Secret scores can hide discrimination, unfairness, and bias. Trade secrets have a place, but secrecy that hides racism, denies due process, undermines privacy rights or prevents justice does not belong anywhere.

Broader transparency for consumer scores with limited confidentiality may offer a middle ground. Knowing the elements but not necessarily the weights of a scoring system provides a partial degree of openness and reassurance. Knowing that there is a scoring system and how and when it is used helps. Knowing the source and reliability of the information used to make a score helps. Being able to challenge a score and correct the data on which it is based helps. Knowing that some types of information will not be used for scoring helps.

Knowing that data collected for one purpose will not be used for another or in violation of law helps. Knowing that the person running the scoring system is accountable in a meaningful way helps. The history of the credit score provides a useful model for the new batch of predictive consumer scores.

Developed in the 1950s, the credit score became part of consumer credit granting. The credit score was mostly secret to the customers that it scored and affected until 2000 when a long and well-documented history of improper uses and abuses finally culminated in the credit score is made available to consumers. Eventually, public pressure caused the credit score's use and even its underlying factors to become public. The use of factors such as race, gender, and religion was prohibited, and this was spelled out in law.

No similar protections exist for most consumer scores today. Consumer scores are today where credit scores were in the 1950s.

Data brokers, merchants, government entities, and others can create or use a consumer score without notice to customers. For various reasons laws governing credit scores do not typically extend protection to the new consumer scores. We need rules that will make consumer scores fair, accountable, accurate, transparent, and non-discriminatory.

This report discusses and explores consumer scores, what goes into them and how they are made, how they are used, the regulations in place that control some but not newest consumer scores, and how scores affect broader privacy and fairness issues. The discussion of findings and recommendations points toward solutions and reforms that are needed.

The History of Scoring

How the Credit Score and Consumer Scores Began, and Why It is relevant today?

The credit score is the progenitor of all consumer scores. The scoring story begins in 1941 with credit scoring and continues today with the broadening of scoring to encompass consumer scoring in finance, insurance, health, and more.

Importance of Credit Scores/Wealth Scores

How does it work?

Whenever you apply to a financial organization for credit such as a loan, credit card or mortgage, they may 'credit score' you. It helps them decide whether to say 'yes' or 'no' to your application. Credit scoring is a system that looks at how your other, similar accounts have been performing and based on this; it predicts what might happen with your credit account. Points are awarded to all the relevant parts of your application and then added together. It's this final score that counts. We use it to assess the risk involved in giving you credit. And then decide whether we can go ahead and accept your application.

Characteristic is included as a factor in the scoring model. This is a much-debated area of scoring.

Raw Consumer Data in the Digital Age. The carefully selected scoring factors and the much-debated weights for standardized credit scores as discussed above are like a landscaped garden in a well -tended public park compared to the untamed jungles of the data factors available and used in the new consumer scores. The new kinds of consumer scores use a much wider array of data sources, to the point that the new data sources make traditional credit scores look under - sourced by comparison.

Whether 500 factors result in a better algorithm than five factors are unknown, and the answer may vary from score to score. More may be better sometimes, but not all the time.

Data for consumer scores can come from many sources, including data broker lists, retail purchases, social scores, census tract data, purchasing patterns, health conditions, ethnicity, book purchasing patterns, exercise patterns, and many other factors.

Data used may be individual to a consumer or model (e.g., all consumers in a census tract). As described above, the effectiveness of a model depends on its ability to predict accurately from a variety of real-world datasets and designated factors. Understanding what a model is trying to predict, what data is used for testing, and how the elements mesh to achieve a result are important to assessing the value, impact, and potential pitfalls of the scoring model. In some cases, it may be that a model is equally effective with less information, negating the need for collection and storage of vast quantities of information and data that could have privacy implications.

Credit Reports

If you have had a loan or credit account with a lender, the lender has probably reported activity on your account to a credit bureau. The three major credit bureaus (Experian, Equifax & TransUnion) are typically what most believe to be a major factor in one's credit worthiness along with employment, collateral, education, capital resources and credit scores that there is an obscure list of consumer data aggregators (CDAs) that credit bureaus own or reference to sell relative data about consumers to provide even more insight to lenders, banks &, etc. Since lenders may not transfer account activity to all credit bureaus, your credit report may vary among credit bureaus. This metric can be called "Fourth Score" or the "Wealth Score Quotient" This "Wealth Score Quotient" has been utilized by most financial institutions in conjunction with the credit reports provided by the big three credit bureaus.

Therefore, it is important to check your credit report annually with each of the three credit bureaus. Contact information is as follows:

Equifax: http://www.equifax.com

Experian: http://www.experian.com/consumer/index.html

TransUnion: http://www.transunion.com/

WEALTH SCORE QUOTIENT:

(noted by Chex Systems)

Understanding Your Credit Score

What are credit scores?

ChexSystems

Simply put, a credit score is a numeric measure of how well you've managed your credit obligations (debt) over time. It was designed for use in loan decisions, but it now has implications in many areas, including:

Insurance (Auto, Home, Life, etc.). Your credit score may be a factor in the calculation of your insurance premium.

Utilities (Gas, Water, Electricity, Cellular, etc.). Without a good credit score, you may be subject to a higher security deposit, which will need to be paid before getting your utilities connected.

Many employers now incorporate your credit score or profile to determine your eligibility for employment.

Special Financing Offers without a good credit score; you will not likely be able to qualify for special offers such as "no interest/no payments until..." that you see advertised on television.

There are hundreds of variations or types of credit scores, which doesn't make understanding them any easier. But all credit score calculations award points for good behavior, and subtract points for bad behavior – so the higher the score, the better.

Scoring Models: How the Consumer Scores Are Made

Just as underlying factors going into a score should be fair and accurate, the algorithms that analyze the information should be of high quality, should generate an accurate prediction and should be validated against real-world data. As models are ultimately judged on their ability to make useful predictions from data, understanding how they perform and against what data sets are essential. Without constant validation, scores might have no actual predictive value in reality. An inadequate or ineffective model ultimately means that the score does not offer accurate predictions. Bad scores based on a faulty or overfit model can still affect the treatment of individual consumers, the most important being eligibility and health care availability decisions.

Score creators have a good reason to get their models right. The marketplace is likely to weed out bad models, although it may take considerable time before this happens. The effects on individuals of poorly predictive consumer scores are uncertain.

It would be useful for model makers to disclose their assumptions, predictive accuracy and model limitations. If a model is inherently a bad predictor of something important, then model users and model data subjects will want to know. Is it the data, the assumptions, overfitting, or other issues?

Good faith, robust, public dialogue here could be helpful to all parties.

Credit score type in the United States – the FICO score.

You've probably heard of credit scoring. Most of the bigger financial organisations use it to work out whether they should lend money to people who apply for credit.

Credit scoring, sometimes called risk scoring, is a rating by a credit bureau to determine your credit worthiness and the likelihood and timeliness of loan repayment. A credit score may impact whether or not you receive credit as well as other credit terms such as percent interest rate, etc.

This booklet aims to remove some of the mystery and explain how credit scoring works, how we use it, how it affects you, and what you can do if you think something's not right.

Your Credit Score

Ultimately, experts say that it is best to have one to three major credit cards, and no more than that. You should keep your balances as low as possible. If you have a credit account with a zero balance, do not close the account.

Instead, make a small purchase, so the card shows up as an active account on your credit report, and you will be awarded points for your long-term credit history.

These are just a few tips to consider as you seek to obtain mortgage financing. But you should always know that as your loan originator, my job is just beginning when you close your loan with me.

As soon as you begin to make mortgage payments on time and in full, your credit standing will begin to improve. My team and I will continue to monitor rates on your behalf and alert you to the opportunity to refinance into a loan program with a lower interest rate as soon as possible. Our long-term goal is to help you build a strong financial future.

CONSIDERATION FACTORS OF A CREDIT SCORE BY LENDERS

Lenders consider several factors of your credit score before extending credit. Equifax, Experian and TransUnion determine a credit score based on a formula developed by the Fair Isaac Corporation. Each credit bureau uses a different term for their credit score. Equifax calls their score "Beacon"; Experian calls their score "FICO"; and the Trans Union calls their score "Empirical".

Again, since lenders do not usually report account activity to all credit bureaus, a credit score may vary among the three credit bureaus. Credit scores may range from 400 to 900 with the average around 700. According to the scoring model, as your score increases, your risk of default decreases.

Vantage Score

The three national credit bureaus have jointly developed the VANTAGE score, which is also a popular credit score. The Vantage scor is regulated under the Fair Credit Reporting Act.

Credit scorecard

Variable	Value/Range	WoE	Estimate	Wald stat	p value	Scoring	Rounded scoring
Balance of Current Account	no running account	-81.810	0.00932	51.19893	0.00000	20.575	21
Balance of Current Account	no balance	-40.139	0.00932	51.19893	0.00000	31.781	32
Balance of Current Account	<= $300	104.229	0.00932	51.19893	0.00000	70.604	71
Balance of Current Account	>$300	104.229	0.00932	51.19893	0.00000	70.604	71
Balance of Current Account	Neutral value	.	.			47.062	47
Duration of Credit	(-inf,9>	75.377	0.00277	1.20626	0.27207	48.600	49
Duration of Credit	(9,15>	38.549	0.00277	1.20626	0.27207	45.656	46
Duration of Credit	(15,30>	-10.834	0.00277	1.20626	0.27207	41.709	42
Duration of Credit	(30,36>	-61.368	0.00277	1.20626	0.27207	37.670	38
Duration of Credit	(36,inf)	-91.629	0.00277	1.20626	0.27207	35.252	35
Duration of Credit	Neutral value	.	.			42.491	42
Payment of Previous Credits	paid back	73.374	0.00750	14.59009	0.00013	58.454	58
Payment of Previous Credits	hesistant	-123.407	0.00750	14.59009	0.00013	15.869	16
Payment of Previous Credits	problematic running accounts	-123.407	0.00750	14.59009	0.00013	15.869	16
Payment of Previous Credits	no previous credits	-8.787	0.00750	14.59009	0.00013	40.674	41
Payment of Previous Credits	no problems with current credits	-8.787	0.00750	14.59009	0.00013	40.674	41
Payment of Previous Credits	Neutral value	.	.			43.541	44
Purpose of Credit	other	-35.920	0.01100	17.13579	0.00003	31.174	31
Purpose of Credit	new car	77.384	0.01100	17.13579	0.00003	67.136	67
Purpose of Credit	furniture	41.006	0.01100	17.13579	0.00003	55.590	56
Purpose of Credit	repair	-60.614	0.01100	17.13579	0.00003	23.337	23
Purpose of Credit	retraining	-23.052	0.01100	17.13579	0.00003	35.258	35
Purpose of Credit	used car	-10.286	0.01100	17.13579	0.00003	39.310	39

In its simplest form, a scorecard is built from some characteristics (that is, input or predictor variables).

Each characteristic includes some attributes. For example, age is a characteristic, and "25-33" is an attribute. Each attribute is associated with some scorecard points. These scorecard points are statistically assigned to differentiate risk, based on the predictive power of the characteristic variables, the correlation between the variables, and business considerations.

For example, using the example Scorecard in Figure ..., an applicant who is 35, makes $38,000 and is a homeowner would be accepted for credit by this financial institution's scorecard. The total score of an applicant is the sum of the scores for each attribute that is present in the scorecard. Lower scores imply a higher risk of default, and upper scores indicate a lower risk of default.

5 FACTORS USED IN DETERMINING A CREDIT SCORE:

There are five basic factors that constitute a credit score. Those factors are outlined here:

Payment History

Approximately 35% of a credit score may be based upon payment history. A credit score is negatively impacted if bills are paid late or if there is a history of delinquent payments listed on the credit report, including matters of public record such as bankruptcy, collection accounts, etc.

Amounts Owed

Approximately 30% of a credit score may be based upon amounts owed or other outstanding debt. A credit score can be negatively impacted if the amount owed is close to the credit limit. A low balance on two credit cards may be better than a high balance on one credit card.

The Length of Credit History

Approximately 15% of a credit score may be based on the length of credit history. A credit score can be positively impacted the longer that accounts have been open, especially if they are with one financial institution.

Taking on More Debt

Approximately 10% of a credit score may be based upon how much new debt a consumer is incurring. A credit score may be negatively impacted if someone has recently applied for some new credit accounts.

Promotional inquiries usually do not negatively impact a credit score.

Types of Credit Score in Use:

Approximately 10% of a credit score may be based upon the types of credit currently in use by a consumer. A credit score is usually negatively impacted by loans from finance companies.

When a lender receives a credit score from the credit bureau, there will be reasons included that explain the score. If the lender rejects a request for credit, and the credit score was part of the reason, the reasons help the lender explain why the score was not higher. Credit score reasons are also useful in determining whether or not a credit report contains errors and how a consumer's credit health might be improved.

1. Paid credit score reports
2. free credit score reports

Who Uses the Credit Score?

- Lenders – Decision AND Pricing (rates)

- Credit Offers – some are good!

- Insurance companies – risk rate policies

- Utility/cell phone companies

- Landlords

- Employers

- Military – Security Clearance

Best Ways to Build Credit

- Low-limit credit card

- Limit the number of credit applications

- Share-secured loan

- Co-borrower or co-signer

- Never charge more than you can pay off in full

- Pay on time or early

Cleaning Up Derogatory Credit

- Keep current accounts current

- Pay newest collections first

- Make a spending plan

- Identify how much can go to clean up

- Contact creditors if unable to make minimum payment, before going delinquent Maintaining/Rebuilding Credit

Manage credit cards carefully!!

- Keep balances below 20% of limit

- Pay down but don't close the card

- No more than seven cards open

- Resist the department store card opening deals

- When closing cards, keep card open the longest

- Careful with the 0% card transfer game

Making Money w/Credit Cards

- Be able to live without credit cards
- Look for rewards cards...5% gas; 3% groceries; King Soopers, etc.
- Pay off balance on time every month!
- Watch the fees

Refinancing Strategies

- Does not hurt the credit score!

- Save money with a lower rate and payment

- No cost

- Easy as a phone call

- Get your score – required score disclosure

- Equity? Consider a cash-out refinance and pay down those high rate cards

What If I Have No Credit?

On occasion, borrower's will not have enough credit references to obtain the loan they wish to secure. If this is the case for you, start by opening small lines of credit that report to all three major CRAs, and make purchases that can be paid off easily. If you do not already have a checking or savings account, open one. Your bank or credit union may be able to provide you with a credit card account once you have established a history with them as a customer.

If you do not have established credit, you are not completely out of luck. Some lenders will pull a report that will show them whether or not consumers pay their rent and utility bills on time. If they like what they see, they may approve you for credit. That is why it is extremely important to pay these day-to-day living expenses on time. Also, your ability to hold a steady job will improve the likelihood of being approved for credit.

It is also wise to start saving money for the down payment on your home. The lender will look at your application more favorably when you can come to the table with a 20% down payment. Bear in mind; there are certain loan programs available that permit a percentage of gift money for down payment. Dealing with Credit Challenges, Unfortunately, a person with a bad credit score is often in this position because he or she lacks the discipline to pay bills on time. Of course, there are exceptions where unforeseen circumstances come into play, such as health complications, or loss of employment. There are a few things that may be able to bring your score up so that you can secure a better interest rate on your mortgage loan.

Example 1:

Distribute debt from revolving credit.

Our borrower, Mr Jones, has a credit score of 664. He has five credit cards, but his Visa account is almost maxed out. His other four credit cards have relatively low balances. Mr Jones moves part of the debt from the Visa account to the other major credit card accounts, thus distributing the debt more evenly over the five cards. This changes the ratio of debt to available credit (which has a 30% impact on the overall credit score), and Mr Jones successfully raises his credit score by 20 points with very little effort. It's important to note that when making balance transfers like these, you should make sure that the balances-to-limit ratios are kept under 30% if you are planning to get a loan shortly. Also note that if transferring monies from one card to others bring any of these balances over 50% of the limit, your credit score will drop.

Example 2:

Transfer outstanding balances to new accounts.

Our borrower, Mr Morgan, has only two credit cards, but both are pushing the limit of available credit. Mr Morgan opens two new credit card accounts, each with a credit limit of $5,000. He transfers part of his existing balances to the new accounts. While he has acquired two new cards that have no established history, the greater impact is the change in the ratio of debt to available credit.

USES OF CONSUMER SCORES, REGULATION, AND MODERN ELIGIBILITY

After a consumer is scored, ranked, described, or classified, companies, governments, private enterprises, health care entities, and others including law enforcement, can then use the resulting score to make decisions about an individual or group.

This is why scores impact consumers every day. Scores are gaining footholds as part of routine business processes for an expanding number of purposes for everything from marketing to assessing a person's identity to predicting a person's likelihood to commit fraud and more. The consumer score acts as a form of predictive evaluation to measure, predict, and facilitate making a decision about things such as an individual's:

- Credit worthiness,
- Popularity,
- Reputation,
- Wealth,
- Propensity to purchase something or default on a loan,
- Measure health,
- Measure/predict likelihood to commit fraud,
- Measure/predict identity
- Measure/predict energy consumption
- Job success probability
- County Court Judgments (number)

- Purpose of loan
- Type of occupation (coded)
- Marital status (married, divorced, single, widow, other)
- Time with bank (years)
- Time with employer (years)
- In the U.S., commonly used predictive variables for traditional financial scoring include:
- Payment history
- Public record and collection items
- Delinquencies
- Prior credit performance
- Outstanding debts
- Relationship between total balances of credit and total limit
- Age of oldest trade line
- Pursuit of new credit (applications to obtain additional credit)
- Time at present address
- Time with current employer
- Type of residence
- Occupation

From these two examples, we see that characteristics included in a financial score model vary from country to country. They may vary from state to state, depending on whether laws restrict the use of some characteristics or variables. The data available in different countries may differ, and that may explain in part the construction of the model. It is not unusual for missing information to be actual.

WEALTH SCORE

CREDIT SCORE

A credit score is a digital representation of a credit file based primarily on any degree, representing the reliability of the character. Your credit score is based on credit basics, usually in new credit.

Creditors, banks and credit scoring agencies use credit ratings to allow potential customers to be shot for money and to reduce losses due to finance. Use credit scores to determine the loan interest rate for qualified lenders, and what credit score limits. Creditors may use credit ratings to determine which customers receive maximum profits. Credit or access before credit rating or credible identity.

Your credit score is not subject to bank restrictions. With the same technology for companies, insurance companies, landlords, other mobile phone companies and government departments. Corporate virtual lenders and simple additions to the Ministry of Finance use the alternative information to calculate the reliability of borrowers. Using a similar technique, the credit score is also consistent with the mining record. Comparable However, these steps are similar or related to thousands of techniques.

In the United States, the credit score is based on a statistical analysis of the personal credit status to represent the credibility of

54

the person's theory, which is expected to be due to the payment of bills. The credit score is mainly based on credit reporting information, usually the main credit bureau three: Experian, TransUnion, and Equifax. Do not take into account the benefits of the main credit bureau when calculating credit ratings.

There is a way to calculate your credit score. Credit score, the most famous credit score system credit score development credit, for the first time known as the company's fair. Many mortgagees use it to determine the likelihood of using a risk-based system, which may be a breach of the borrower's financial obligations. All credit ratings are based on availability. Credit Bureau has its credit rating: Equifax Scorepower (Equifax), credit score Equifax Experian, TransUnion credit score and VantageScore credit score are familiar. Also, large lenders, including many credit card issuers, have developed their proprietary scoring models.

The results show that the forecast and bond underwriting risk insurance. The study also shows that most consumers are beneficiaries of premiums due to the use of low-cost credit and insurance credit scores.

Credit score advanced by way of agencies inclusive of score logic probe, l2c, Innovis, and so on within the final decade who predict the certification bureau. The credit rating of jss score logic makes use of a specific set of risk factors, including the borrower's present paintings, income, income, the effect of the economy, forecasting of credit score hazard, thus increasing your credit rating. Those new varieties of credit score scores are frequently enhancing the precision of mixture forecasts with FICO rating or bureau. Maximum creditors nowadays use an aggregate of credit score bureau rating and alternative outcomes to expand a better know-how of the capability to pay. It is known that Fico has a degree of potential to pay. Credit rating focusing potential to pay within the future to focus more on deploying to boom mortgage threat model. L2c gives alternative credit rating makes the carrier records to decide the credentials and after many creditors use this rating similarly to the credit bureau selections. Many lenders use of jss score logic score plus the bureau, thinking about the jss result determines the activity stability and income that must be able to pay off the loan in the future. It is thought that the fico score will continue to be the result however it's miles expected to serve as a combined with other opportunity credit scores to provide different images of hazard.

All three credit score bureaus are eligible to receive an unfastened credit file inside any December, but they may be no longer entitled to a free credit score. The three credit score bureaus can run an annual credit report. Com, wherein customers get unfastened credit reviews. The credit score can be used as an extra feature of the file, charging costs. If the client dispute does no longer assure a credit file below the task not a document of the credit act (store), the credit bureau gets a forty-five-day investigation instead of 30 days for the record.

Also, consumers want to get their credit rating in a few instances; you may buy them one at a time from the credit bureau or purchase their credit score immediately from FIGO. Credit scoring (including credit score scoring) can also be subscribed free to consolidate credit score card organizations or other 0.33 parties with multiple credit score reporting monitoring services, notwithstanding the reality that the unfastened score of such offerings is obtained, the signing of subscription carrier free trial you must use the credit score card before the primary month of price is made and cancelled. Like wallet hub, sesame, credit score enterprise credit website gives loose credit scoring, no credit score card necessities the use of VantageScore version 3.0 the TransUnion.

Fashionable or traditional credit score three hundred 850. VantageScore rating range from three.0 to three hundred-850. The old VantageScore is among 501 and 990.

The first step in explaining the score is to decide the credit score and the supply of its use. There are numerous special scoring ratings based on version escort and others. The maximum commonplace is created using Figo's rating and analyzing. Figo is an indexed business enterprise (Nasdaq) is the maximum well-known, most extensively used credit score version established in the USA. Within the "credit score rating model" issued by using the three curators (Equifax Canada and TransUnion Canada) of us national debt (The TransUnion, Equifax, and Experian), this version was set up in a distribution organization by using countrywide treasury bonds. Credit manage the maximum of the marketplace credit scores of the united states, and Canada has some players, other competition proportion a totally small percentage of the market.

The credit risk score (prescribed layout motive) is expected to set the probability of performance; the customer score has been calculated for 90 days or awful purpose to enter the month. The better the score, the much less possibly he or she is., loans for diverse uses (mortgages, motors, credit cards) have one-of-a-kind parameters, adjusted by the auto. To this cease, at the same time as evaluating the loan score, the credit score rating on the credit card credit score card.

Many factors affect a person's credit rating. Saul's element as compared to the total loan character as someone. One borrows, or levers, money, and reduces the balance of guy.

The maximum popular credit scoring models and their obstacles:

Phillips rating: three hundred-850

VantageScore 3. Zero: three hundred-850

VantageScore (1. Zero and a pair of. Zero variations): 501-990

Bonus factors: 330-830

Transunion (trans risk): 100-900

Simulation: Experian national score 360-840

Equifax: 280-850

Creditxpert: 300-900

Scoresense: 350-850.

CREDIT SCORE IN THE UNITED STATES

The credit score rating of America is represented with the aid of the reputation of someone who pays his or her money owed.

Creditors, inclusive of banks and credit agencies, use credit score scores to assess the potential risks to customers due to investment. Widespread use of credit score scoring credits is extra broadly available and cheaper for many customers.

CREDIT SCORING MODELS

FICO score

The credit score version is used by most banks and credit card groups for presents and underneath the three-credit country patron credit bureaus: Experian, Equifax, and the TransUnion. For a reason that customer credit bureau's file may additionally have different information on each score, the credit score can be generated wherein the bureau gives the Phillips.

THE MAKEUP OF CREDIT

The credit rating account is supposed to measure the risk of default via contemplating various factors in the private financial scenario. Even though the calculated credit rating has a correct formulation mystery, FICO has been informed of the subsequent components.

35%: charge history: is defined as the first-rate appearance or lacks convincing statistics. Financial ruin, lien, choice, agreement, disgusting charge, bailout, foreclosure, overdue payment may also purpose FICO to skip the result.

30%: debt burden: this sort of credit score takes into consideration a few unique measurements. Consistent with FICO, there are 6 one of a kind indicator inside the mortgage class, consisting of the quota ratio, the stability of the stability, the exceptional quantity between the one of a kind styles of bills and the quantity paid using the installment mortgage.

15%: the length of the credit score record in the file is likewise known as time: credit score history and age, like this, will have a positive impact on your score FICO. This category includes two indicators: the common age of the account within the document, the age of the vintage account.

10%: the sort of credit used (recycle chapters, customer finance, mortgages): clients can revel in the history of handling distinct sorts of loans.

10%: Either seek recently: while a client applies for a credit card or loan (or other) takes place while a difficult credit query, the result may be harm, mainly if the huge amount. In a quick time, frame (two weeks or 45 days, based on the fico score), mortgages, vehicle loans or loans who are suffering "purchasing" cannot be extensively reduced through those kinds of queries because the fico version scores every weight those varieties of link exams occur in 14 days or forty-five days in an afternoon, similar to one. Similarly, while the FICO score is much less than 30 days, mortgages, car loans, and scholar mortgage inquiries aren't relied upon at all. While all credit checks could be recorded and submitted for two years in the personal credit document, they will be effective for the reason that first year because the fico scoring approach became unnoticed after 12 months. The patron's behavior of a credit score take a look at (inclusive of a stretched private credit document), an enterprise (employee verification), or a default corporation providing credit or insurance has no effect on the credit score rating display referred to as "smooth take a look at" or "gentle pull" on the credit score report used by the lender, only to the personal document. The credit score rating technique does no longer take into account the gentle query.

OTHER CREDIT SCORES

Non-credit score rankings are referred to as "credits" for some academic or fake ratings. The edition] Experian credit score is an educational use (more factor) handiest among 330 and 830, scores Experian plus the score is between three hundred and 900. Equifax credit score between 280 and 850. A few lenders use scores from a hundred to 990 packages that explain the credit score optical evaluation take a look at between 1 and 999. Transunion trans risk website is the brand-new account in the credit karma among 300 and 850, 840 from the country wide credit score Experian 360 sesame and credits. Com variety. Lenders do not use many web sites (Equifax, TransUnion, credit score, Moore, and so forth.) offer one-of-a-kind credit score rankings to clients, but they. Chex systems customer 100 cents from 899, credit score from public a hundred to 850, and the vocabulary rating to derive reinsurance 500 out of 997.

Free annual credit report

Due to actual behavior (honest and correct credit score transaction law), every legitimate American resident is suitable for a credit file or credit score reporting corporation each ten month. The regulation calls for all three groups, **Equifax, Experian, TransUnion**, to offer reviews. These credit reports do no longer have credit score ratings from all three corporations. The three credit bureaus can run an annual credit report. Com, in which users get unfastened credit score reports. Non-credit score scoring is the value of reporting as an additional function. The fee is typical $7.95, just as the FTC exceeded the correct credit score-reporting invoice for charging policies.

Non-traditional uses of credit scores

Credit rating is normally used to decide car costs, landlord insurance. The country wide credit score reporting organization, which produces a credit score also has an extra specific coverage rating, which is a butcher created using an insurance corporation for potential customer insurance dangers. Studies show that most people's insurance rates are lower than the insurance ratings. These research display that excessive scores of human beings declare much less.

Use in employment decisions

Equifax, TransUnion, Experian, an enterprise association (the customer facts enterprise association or C" DIA") are lacking. The employer does no longer receive a credit score for the employment document of the loan sale document. All international locations are allowed to use credit reporting for process screening, despite the fact that a few humans have already accomplished so. The criminal restrictions on the practice are only a few data.

Free annual credit report

Because of authentic behavior (fair and accurate credit transaction law), every legitimate American resident is appropriate for a credit report or credit score reporting enterprise every ten months. The law calls for all three agencies, Equifax, Experian, Transunion, to provide reviews. These credit reviews do no longer have credit scores from all three agencies. The three credit bureaus can run an annual credit report. Com, wherein users get free credit score reviews. Non-credit score scoring is the fee of reporting as a further characteristic. This is usually 7.95 dollars, the usage of the proper credit score and reporting invoice to the charging path.

THE CREDIT BUREAUS

The credit score card organization collects the credit account of the records collection enterprise and offers this data to the purchaser reporting organization in the America, UK credit record, credit in Australia, first credit score in India Corp. (CIC) And the Philippines are in particular quasi-stakes. This isn't the same as the credit rating corporations.

A CONSUMER REPORTING AGENCY

Customer reporting organizations are presenting information and borrowing to pay their bills. Loan statistics, such as people's present-day loans, is an effective device for predicting destiny conduct. These establishments reduce the effect of asymmetric facts between debtors and lenders and reduce the impact and moral troubles. As an example, information on appropriate loans may want to make it less difficult for lenders to borrow, monitor and discover, and keep away from high-threat loans. It suggests lenders comparing credit score competencies, having the ability to repay loans, which can affect interest costs and different loan positions. Everyone's hobby costs are identical, but on the contrary, based totally on danger pricing, different lenders may also set up their credit score rating based on the anticipated danger of a shape of fee discrimination. Clients with credit score responsibilities as an awful credit history or a tax lien on criminal soundness or financial disaster pay excessive annual hobby rates than clients who aren't these factors. Also, all choice-makers in regions unrelated to purchase loans encompass underwriting of coverage belongings and reliance on credit score agreements, as research shows that these facts may be expected. At the equal time, clients also gain from credit score information systems as it reduces the effect of monopolistic banks with the aid of supplying debtors with incentives to pay off their debts over time.

In the U.S.A., client reporting companies accumulate and aggregate personal information, monetary statistics and information reporting groups to gain relationships called numerous facts sources, however people. Formatted information normally lenders, lenders, utilities, debt series corporations (credit score bureaus) and courts (i.e., Public facts) patron with courting or enjoy. Format facts review credit score reporting agencies charge clients. The information supplied by those inns, in addition to information buffers collected with the aid of the FBI, or files from purchaser reporting organizations. The records generated is a client reporting enterprise that assesses credit hazard, credit scoring purposes, or ideas for different purposes, inclusive of employment or condominium leasing. Given the large wide variety of consumer debtors, these credit scoring mechanisms. To streamline the patron analysis manner, the purchaser reporting employer's mathematical set of rules gives a consumer score to evaluate the probability that the man or woman will pay off the loan due to the fact they may be regularly given to others in comparable situations. Maximum client welfare advocates propose people to study a credit score document every year to make sure they're proper.

BUSINESS CREDIT REPORTING AGENCIES

Enterprise credit score reports and scoring bureaus also exist, and a commercial enterprise fee may be used to assess the probability of creditors. Examples of business credit reports are pay ex-fractions a result of world credit score services, CIC coordinates, Affiliation credit reporting countrywide debt control Association's country wide change. Equifax TransUnion is likewise an instance of the rapid rating of global and industrial credit reporting organizations.

In the U.S.A., there may be no legal term inside the credit enterprise underneath the ideal federal credit reporting act (keep). Consumer reporting groups are typically easy industries.

Within the united states, the main customer reporting groups diagnosed patron protection facilities, trendy consumer reporting businesses or other commercial enterprise statistics, upholstery is the appropriate federal credit reporting act (rescue), honest and correct credit score regulation (press beatings), appropriate credit score invoice (FCBA).

Different government corporations screen Agency reporting corporations and proportion duties with people who send them.

The federal change fee (FTC), consumer reporting employer, changed into examined. The alternate treaty (OCC) is the workplace of the controller and is chargeable for the control and supervision of all countrywide financial institution statistics files on client reporting businesses.

WEALTH SCORE CALCULATOR

This calculator is designed to give you a "Wealth Score" similar to how a credit score (like FICO) is calculated.

Score Range: 300-850

EXCELLENT 775+ - Prodigious Accumulators of Wealth (PAW), exceeding wealth target (>200%)

GOOD 675-774 - On pace with wealth target (100-200%)

FAIR 625-674 - Near wealth target (50-99%)

POOR 575-624 - Under Accumulator of Wealth (UAW), well short of wealth target (<50%)

VERY POOR <575 - Under Accumulator of Wealth (UAW), negative net worth.

This formula is age income / 10 = wealth target. I like this formula because it accounts for inflation effects. And compensates for age. It does not, however, account for trajectory over time and is just a snapshot in time. Especially with younger workers, a downward trajectory with debts can be more important than net worth. This formula also does not account for sudden large increases or reductions in income. According to https://www.nabber.org/projects/wealthscore/

2. What's Your Wealth Score?

We can do this by digging through the figures in the newly released 1998 Survey of Consumer Finances. The survey is done every three years by the Federal Reserve Board to check on our collective financial condition and see how our habits are changing.

Here is how the scoring works

The survey breaks us down into five groups:

- Those in the bottom 25 percent of the wealth pyramid,
- The 25 percent just below the midpoint of the wealth pyramid,
- The 25 percent just above the midpoint of the wealth pyramid,
- Those who range from the top 25 percent to the top 10 percent,
- And the top 10 percent of all families.

Having established the categories, the analysts then go through the survey results and find the median value of each type of wealth holding. In other words, half the people in each group will have more, and half will have less, of any particular asset type. The survey, for instance, shows that those in the bottom 25 percent of the wealth pyramid have median transaction account assets of $600 while those in the top 10 percent have median transaction account assets of $23,000. As you always suspected, some people have more in their checking accounts than others.

They do the same thing for debts. The figures show, for instance, that credit card balances are very evenly distributed. Our friends with all the stamps and mailing lists have made it as easy for the bottom 25 percent of the population to owe $1,600 as they have for the top 10 percent to owe $2,000. While these figures are all medians and can't be construed to represent exactly how each group is faring, it's probably safe to say that people in the bottom half don't have a lot of equity in their homes while people in the top half have a good deal of equity.

How do you score yourself?

Examine the figures in each column and check the one that seems to apply to you. Chances are you'll find that most fall in one of the columns and, barring other asset ownership such as a private business, you're probably in that percentile range.

However, are there any surprises?

Most people who are affluent, I've found, have no idea just how high up the wealth scale they are. If you've owned a modestly upscale home in any city, been married, worked down your debt, and both you and your spouse have been contributing to a qualified savings plan over the last ten years, you've got a very good chance of being in the top ten percent.

Note, please, the lack of miracles, hot tips, or savvy investments in technologies that require a Ph.D. to understand. It all starts with spending less than you earn.

3. The Wealth Rating

You can now view overall wealth rating information of accounts in your database from Target Analytics, a division of Blackbaud Inc

Target Analytics screens your individuals and prospects located in the United States based on public assets, including:

High-confidence real estate ownership, based on their name and address

Private company information, based on their reported ownership percentage

High-confidence public company insider holdings and options

Then, Target Analytics ranks your individuals and prospects on their wealth data up to five stars. The higher the wealth rating, the higher the stars. With this information, you can determine where to focus your fundraising energies and who to ask for larger gifts. For example, these are a recommendation you assign your four- and five-star constituents to an attentive fundraiser with more care and interaction than other donors.

A five-star constituent has public assets greater than USD 25,000,000.

A four-star constituent has public assets between $10,000,000 and $25,000,000 USD.

A three-star constituent has public assets between $1,000,000 and $10,000,000 USD.

A two-star constituent has public assets between $500,000 and $1,000,000 USD.

A one-star constituent has public assets up to USD 500,000.

If Target Analytics cannot accurately identify a constituent or screen their wealth, they appear with No rating.

Tip: System Administrators that use the Essentials or Pro package of eTapestry in the United States can take advantage of this new service two times per year. For questions about the Essentials and Pro packages of eTapestry and eTapestry subscriptions. This data appears on the Data Health Scorecard as well as the new Wealth Rating tile on the Account Home page. You can also query and report on wealth data to analyze relevant information for your organization.

Wealth Rating Data Health Score

The Wealth Rating Data Health Score tile displays on the Home page when you open eTapestry. The information that appears in this section varies depending on your wealth rating data's current state. For example, basic wealth rating information displays with a link to learn more details about the service before you run it for the first time.

When an extended period has passed since you last ran the service, information appears to remind you to run the service again. To schedule your next service, click the Go to Wealth Rating link on the page.

If you are using eTapestry in the United States, the scorecard tile appears for System Administrators on the Home page dashboard after your database health is analyzed. You can close the file manually or wait for it to disappear after a few days. The report also appears for

System Administrators under Account Reports on the eTapestry Standard Reports page. For all other countries, the report appears for System Administrators under Account Reports on the eTapestry Standard Reports page only.

After you run the service, the information updates, and the scorecard includes the accounts analyzed by the service and their overall wealth ratings. It also includes helpful links to queries for wealth rating data.

Schedule the Service

You can schedule the wealth rating service to run twice a year. To schedule the service, you can select a query of accounts, select a date to run the service, and enter email addresses for those in your organization who should receive summary information after the service completes.

4 Wealth Opportunity Score

Your identity is valuable. We can help protect it.

Get better identity theft detection, protection & resolution from Experian

Note: Free for 30 days, then just $19.99 /month

Start with your free Experian Credit Report

No credit card required. This offer does not include a free Score.

New Experian Credit Report every 30 days

Monitoring of your Experian Credit Report with alerts

Target with unmatched precision

Wealth Opportunity Score is the only wealth-estimation model developed using fresh, comprehensive and direct-measured investable asset data, which provides unmatched accuracy and targeting precision. The score enables data and analytics, strategic planning, and sales and marketing professionals to develop actionable strategies and tactics across the entire Customer Life Cycle, from prospecting to acquisition to cross-selling to retention.

Unmatched data foundation

Unlike other solutions that rely on stale, self-reported data subject to sampling errors and response bias, Wealth Opportunity Score is the only wealth-estimation model developed using verified and direct-measured investor data, reported monthly by more than 800 financial data contributors.

Wealth Opportunity Score was created and is administered by Experian, the global leader for consumer data management, providing expert insights, analytical tools, and marketing services to organizations and consumers. The score was developed using direct-measured investor data from Broadridge® Financial Solutions, the leading provider of proxy voting services for more than 90 percent of banks, broker-dealers, mutual funds, insurance companies and publicly traded corporations in the United States, providing an unmatched competitive advantage.

Unparalleled data granularity

Whether you want to target households with $100,000, $100 million or $1 billion in investable assets, Wealth Opportunity Score provides unparalleled data granularity — asset ranges start in thousand-dollar increments with no caps. The score is calibrated monthly to reflect stock market changes, wealth transfers, and household moves, allowing you to measure progress in target-marketing initiatives and identify new opportunities with unmatched precision.

Comprehensive coverage of consumer wealth

Wealth Opportunity Score leverages Experian's demographic and predictive marketing factors and proprietary advanced analytics techniques to provide an estimate of total household wealth for more than 110 million U.S. households. The score represents a household's total liquid investable wealth, including equities, exchange-traded funds, mutual funds, bonds, money market funds and cash deposits held both at your firm and other firms. This enables you to pinpoint total household financial capacity with the highest precision and to focus resources on households with the greatest opportunity for growth.

Gain a competitive edge

Wealth Opportunity Score gives you a strategic advantage over the competition by enabling you to:

Optimize targeted marketing efforts for wealth-management, brokerage, insurance, and retail-banking products across the entire Customer Life Cycle (acquisition, cross-selling, up-selling and retention)

Create highly customized marketing messages and offers that resonate with your audience

Develop proprietary scores for marketing and business-planning applications

Data-mine your Customer Relationship Management (CRM) database to determine product strategy, customer onboarding, acquisition, loyalty programs and account management

Develop share of wallet and lifetime value measures for current customers and prospects Easy to implement

Wealth Opportunity Score can be delivered in any of the following formats:

Score append to client CRM file

Score append to client-provided prospect list

Experian-generated prospect list based on client specifications

Direct data feed into any Decisioning as a Service marketing module (e.g., Retail bank client cross-sell)

Enter the consumer credit world

Insights and solutions to power your credit decisions

The world of consumer credit can feel complex. After all, our database represents 220 million credit-active consumers nationwide with 1.3 billion updates flowing through monthly. How can a business sort through this enormous dataset to identify consumers, the decision on loans, market to prospects and collect?

Experian's Consumer Information Services division offers a suite of solutions to assist lenders, government entities, retailers and beyond with all aspects of the customer credit lifecycle.

AN EASY, 3-STEP WEALTH SCORE

I recently posted on the formula that The Millionaire Next Door uses to determine what a person's net worth should be. There was lots of discussion over this formula with several people suggesting alternative ideas. So, when I saw this article on Money Central that helps determine a wealth score, I just had to post on it. Here's the summary:

A key ratio -- net worth divided by lifetime earnings -- provides a telling gauge of your financial progress, no matter how big your paycheck.

Here are the details:

Step 1: Add up your lifetime earnings. You don't have to go searching for your old tax returns; just use the handy summary Social Security sends you every year, a few months before your birthday.

Step 2: Calculate your net worth. This measure of wealth is the total of all your assets (investments and property) minus your liabilities (your debt).

Step 3: Divide your net worth by your lifetime earnings. This is what all your labor has achieved for you regarding tangible wealth.

Rick Ulivi, a fee-only financial planner in Orange, Calif., likes to have his clients do this calculation. He wants to see the following ratios:

For young clients early in their careers, the desired ratio is somewhere between 0 and 25%. For clients in mid-career, he wants a ratio between 25% and 100%.

By the time they're ready for retirement, the preferred ratio is 100% to 200%.

Exceeding these ratios is great, of course -- just not very common.

Surprisingly, these calculations were very similar to what some Free Money Finance readers were suggesting. Do you think this is a good way to measure wealth?

WEALTH SCORES AND RATINGS

Wealth Insight Scores

Propensity to Give

Propensity to Spend

Estimated Spending Capacity

Total Assets

Net Worth

Cash on Hand

Estimated Annual Donations

Gift Capacity Range

Wealth Attribute Ratings

Gift Capacity Rating

RFM

Planned Giving—Bequest, Annuity & Trust Influence

Inclination: Giving

Inclination: Affiliation

Predictive Scores Append Documentation

Predictive Scores Append API Overview

Data finder's Predictive Scores Append API service enables you to programmatically score and sort your leads by popular metrics such as a person's wealth, propensity to give, propensity to be green, and more.

Inputs and outputs:

For a complete list of inputs, please see the "Parameters" section. For a full list of outputs, please see the "Output Fields."

Predictive Scores Options

These are scores you may retrieve through the Predictive Scores API. Enter them as a comma separated list in the scores parameter.

https://datafinder.com/api/docs-scores

Fields returned for each record in the "results":

How Wealthy are You now? - Thomas J. Stanley's Wealth Equation Calculator

http://www.hughcalc.org/wealth.cgi

THE WEALTH CALCULATOR

FINANCIAL CALCULATOR, YOU NEED TO KNOW

84

This is a life financial tracking to reveal how far financial freedom you have presently. Check out http://www.hughcalc.org/index.php

GUIDE TO CREDIT SCORING, CREDIT REPORTING AND FRAUD PREVENTION AGENCIES.

Assessing applications for credit

Lenders take into account your personal and business circumstances when opening personal and business accounts or establishing the appropriate level of credit to grant you or your business. Applications may be assessed using a process called credit scoring.

How does credit score work?

Credit scoring takes into account information provided directly by you, any information the lender may hold about you, and any information obtained from other organizations. They use information from other organizations, which may include a licensed Credit Reporting Agency.

The credit scoring system allocates points for each piece of relevant information and adds these up to produce a score. When your score reaches a certain level, then the lender will agree to your application. If your score does not reach this level, they may not. Sometimes scores are calculated by a Credit Reporting Agency and may use these in assessing your application.

The points allocated are based on thorough analysis of large numbers of repayment histories over many years of providing credit. This statistical analysis enables them to identify characteristics that predict. Future performance. For example, individuals who have county court judgments registered in their name have proved to be less likely to meet payments than those without judgments.

Credit scoring produces consistent decisions and is designed to ensure all applicants are treated fairly. Additionally, the lender has policy rules to determine whether they will lend. These reflect their commercial experience and requirements. For example, if they have direct evidence that you have shown poor management of credit products in the past then they may decline your application.

Every application to open an account or borrow money involves some degree of repayment risk for the lender, no matter how reliable or responsible an applicant is. Credit scoring enables us to calculate the degree of risk for each applicant based on the information we have obtained. If the level of acceptable risk to us is exceeded, we will not accept the application. This does not mean that any declined applicant is a bad payer. It simply means that based on the information available to us, we are not prepared to take the risk of opening that account or granting that loan.

Lenders are not obliged to accept an application. Lenders have different lending policies and scoring systems, and so applications to them may be assessed differently. This means that one lender may accept your application but another may not. If your application is declined, this will not be disclosed to the Credit Reporting Agency.

Is Credit Scoring Fair?

We believe that credit scoring is fair and impartial. It does not single out a specific piece of information as the reason for declining an application. We test our credit scoring methods regularly to make sure they continue to be fair and unbiased. Responsible lending is essential both for the good of applicants and lender. Applicants with county court judgments may find credit difficult to obtain.

The Ins and Outs of Credit Scoring

When you want to pay for something quickly and easily, a loan or credit card can come in very handy. But at the same time, you don't want to find the repayments a struggle. That's why we use credit scoring. It helps us make sure you're less likely to get into difficulty – borrowing money you can't afford.

Credit scoring helps us make sure everything is fair. We treat all applications in the same way so that all our customers receive credit impartially. And we constantly check the accuracy of our systems.

How credit agencies work on loan application

So who are these credit agencies that I've mentioned previously? A Credit Reporting Agency gathers and stores financial and public information. It doesn't make decisions about whether you should receive credit, it simply provides factual information to help financial organizations to decide whether to accept your application.

'The public information includes data from the Electoral Register that helps to identify you, plus details of any County Court Judgments or bankruptcies against you.

Altitude of Consumers on Building up their Credit Profile.

Usually, the lender needs just three main pieces of information to build up your profile and give you a credit score:

- The details you gave on your application form

- How you've managed other accounts with them

- Information from a national Credit Reporting Agency

They use all these details about you, such as your age, employment history, any existing credit you have with them and other lenders, to build up your profile. How you've managed previous accounts – plus any other factors that they know to be good indicators of risk, also help.

How does your credit history affect loan application?

Your credit history is made up of information from credit providers or lenders. They share information with each other. So when someone applies for credit, it's possible to check how well a person has repaid the money in the past. If you've always regularly repaid the credit, this will look good on your application. Alternatively, if you weren't able to repay a loan on time, this might have a negative impact.

However, people who have had financial difficulties in the past are more likely to have difficulties keeping up repayments in the future. So if you are already having difficulties, being able to get hold of more credit might not be helpful to you at this time.

How other people can affect you

You may have read in the press about people unfairly being refused credit because someone who once lived at their address or living with has a bad credit history as may sometimes arise as part of the point in rejection, majorly, some do not use this as a reference to refuse approval. It won't be because you've shared the same address. It will only ever be someone you are financially connected with.

What about people you live with?

When you apply for credit with us, we may take into account other members of your household with whom you have some financial connection. For example, it could be someone you share an account with or someone you have made a joint application with for credit in the past.

A credit reporting agency won't provide us with information about someone who used to live at your address just for the sake of it. They will only ever do this if there has been a financial link with you and that other person.

Don't agree with the information about you?

If the details a Credit Reporting Agency holds about you are correct, they can't change them. But of course, if something is wrong, their consumer help service will help you to put it right. And what if a credit reporting agency gives you information about people you live with, but you don't have any financial connection with them? You can change this too. The agency will send you details of your rights under the Consumer Credit Act 1974 and the Data Protection Act 1998 when you apply to see your details.

Maintaining good credit score

1. Always make on-time payments to current loans and credit card balances.

Consider   setting up automatic payments using Bill Pay, or by providing your credit card or debit card number to service providers who bill you on an ongoing basis.

2. Reduce the amount of debt you owe.

You can pay your debt down more quickly if it is at the lowest interest rates available. If you already have a strong score, determine whether or not there are any opportunities for you to refinance some debt at a lower interest rate.

3. Try to maintain a good ratio of the amount borrowed versus the limit on revolving credit lines.

When the percentage of the amount owed is 30% or higher, lenders may see you as using your revolving lines as an extension of your income or not living within your means.

4. Do not apply for credit too often.

Several inquiries in a short period can lower your credit score. Be aware of soft pulls and hard pulls on your credit and do not be afraid to ask the person conducting the credit review how this will affect you.

5. Have a variety of credit included in your profile.

Contacting the big three Credit Reporting Agency and how to request to see your files and access your consumer reports.

When should consumers check the information held about them? Why sometimes lenders refuse credit?

The three main credit bureaus: Equifax, Experian, and TransUnion

1. Equifa

How Equifax works?

2. Experian

How Experian works?

3. TransUnion

How TransUnion works?

FACTORS AFFECTING CONSUMERS APPLICATION FOR CREDIT

The research for this report found that consumer scores may rely on hundreds or thousands of pieces of consumer information coming from many different data sources.

This report identifies a large roster of raw consumer data that includes demographic information like age, race, gender, ethnicity, and home address as well as religion, mobile phone number, online and offline purchase history, health conditions like Alzheimer's, diabetes, and multiple sclerosis, as well as intimate financial details such as net worth, card holder information, low or high-end credit scores, money market funds, ages of children, and a great deal more.

Statistical scoring methods rely on the increasing availability of large amounts of new source data from social media, the web in general, and elsewhere. The input for consumer scores can include information that is mostly unobjectionable or public. But, as discussed, consumer scores also can incorporate highly sensitive information that in other contexts could be used in a prejudicial, unfair, or unethical way in making decisions about consumers.

Some data, such as social media data, can be unobjectionable in one context, but inappropriate as a factor, for example, in credit decisioning models.

An example and a fairly common one is a predictive model that a major US health insurer worked with an analytics company to create. The idea was to determine whether or not publicly available consumer data could enhance the quality and effectiveness of their predictive risk models. They tested approximately 1,500 factors at the household level and found that the consumer information that showed the most value in predicting individual level risk included:

- Age of the Individual

- Gender

- Frequency of purchase of general apparel

- Total amount of inpatient claims

- Consumer prominence indicator

- Primetime television usage

- Smoking

- Propensity to buy general merchandise

- Ethnicity

- Geography – district and region

- Mail order buyer - female apparel

- Mail order buyer - sports goods

DOS AND DON'TS DURING THE LOAN PROCESS.

When you fill out a credit application, we run a credit report for the underwriter. Each lender and each loan program have different guidelines they must follow. You should not do anything that will hurt your credit score while your loan is in the process. We know it's tempting. If you're moving into a new home, you might be thinking about purchasing new appliances or furniture, but this is not the right time to go shopping with your credit cards.

You'll want to remain in a stable position until the loan closes and give us the opportunity to help you lock in the best interest rate we can get for you.

Do's

Most importantly do stay in contact with your mortgage and real estate professionals.

If you have a question about whether or not, you should take a specific action that you believe may affect your credit reports or scores during the loan process, your mortgage or real estate professional may be able to supply you with the resources you need.

Do pay bills on time

Stay current on existing accounts.

Under the new FICO scoring model, one 30-day late can cost you anywhere from 50-100 points, and points lost for late pays take several months if not years to recover.

Don'ts

Don't do anything that will cause a red flag to be raised by the scoring system.

This includes the not-so-obvious things like co-signing on loan or changing a name or address with the bureaus. The less activity on a report during the loan process, the better.

Don't apply for new credit of any kind

Including those "You have been pre-approved" credit card invitations that you receive in the mail or online. Every time that you have your credit pulled by a potential creditor or lender, you lose points from your credit score immediately. New credit also brings a credit score down. Depending on the elements in your current credit report, you could lose anywhere from one to 15 points for one hard inquiry.

Don't pay off collections or charge offs during the loan process.

Unless you can negotiate a deletion letter, paying collections will decrease the credit score immediately due to the date of last activity becoming recent. If you want to pay off old accounts, do it through escrow – at closing.

Don't max out or over charge on your credit card accounts.

In the matter of fact, DON'T charge on credit cards at all if possible. This is the fastest way to bring your scores down 50-100 points immediately. Keep your credit card balances below 30% of their available limit at ALL times during the loan process. And if you decide to pay down balances, do it across the board. Meaning, pay balances to bring your balance to limit ratio to the same level on each card (i.e. all to 30% of the limit, or all to 40%, etc.)

Don't consolidate your debt onto 1 or 2 credit cards

It seems like it would be the smart thing to do, however, when you consolidate all of your debt onto one card, it appears that you are maxed out on that card, and the system will penalize you as mentioned. If you want to save money on credit card interest rates, wait until after closing.

Don't close accounts.

If you close a credit card account, you will lose available credit, and it will appear to FICO that your debt ratio has gone up. Also, closing a card or installment account will affect other factors in the score such as length of credit history. If you HAVE to close an account for DTI plan the time. DO NOT close credit cards until after closing.

Don't allow any accounts to run past due even 1 day!

Most cards offer a grace period, however, what they don't tell you is that once the due date passes, that account will show a past due amount on your credit report. Past due balances can also drop scores by 50+ points.

Don't dispute anything on your credit report

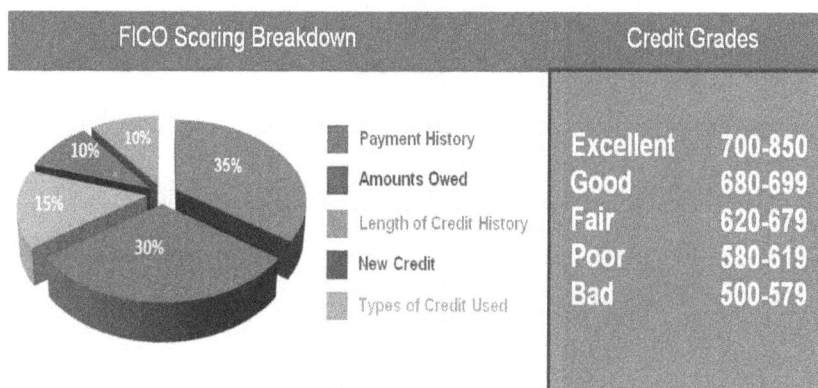

FICO Scoring Breakdown	Credit Grades	
■ Payment History	Excellent	700-850
■ Amounts Owed	Good	680-699
■ Length of Credit History	Fair	620-679
■ New Credit	Poor	580-619
■ Types of Credit Used	Bad	500-579

Once the loan process has started. When you send a letter of dispute to the credit reporting agencies, a note is put onto your credit report, and when the underwriter notices items in dispute, in many instances, they will not process the loan until the note is removed and new credit scores are pulled. Why? Because in some instances, credit scoring software will not consider items in dispute in the credit score – giving false data to the lender.

A well-known credit score is the FICO Score.

There are numerous credit scores, but FICO appears to lead regarding sales. Fair Isaac states:

The FICO Scores is the most widely used credit score in North America. Lenders purchased more than 10 billion FICO Scores in 2013, and 90 percent of all U.S. consumer lending decisions use the FICO Score. The 25 largest credit card issuers, the 25 largest auto lenders and tens of thousands of other businesses rely on the FICO Score for consumer credit risk analysis and federal regulatory compliance."

The FICO score falls squarely under the Fair Credit Reporting Act.

FICO also has an Expansion Score that draws on alternative credit data such as bank account records, payday loan payment records, and installment purchase plans, to produce a credit score that may not be based solely on the consents of a credit report. Other companies also offer similar credit scores for people with "thin" credit reports.

UNDERSTANDING FICO SCORE

If you've ever applied for a credit card, car loan, mortgage or another type of credit, there's a

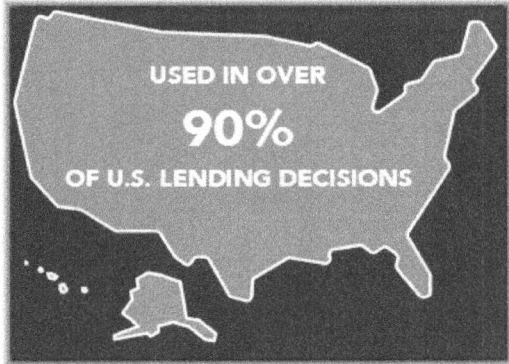

USED IN OVER **90%** OF U.S. LENDING DECISIONS

very good chance your lender used your FICO Scores to help them decide

a) a) Whether to approve you

b) What terms and interest rates you qualify for. That's because FICO Scores are used in over 90% of U.S. lending decisions.

The higher your FICO Scores, the better.

FICO Scores range from 300 to 850, though industry-specific FICO Scores have a slightly broader 250 – 900 score range. Higher FICO Scores demonstrate lower credit risk, and lower FICO Scores demonstrate higher credit risk.

What's considered a "good" FICO Score varies by lender.

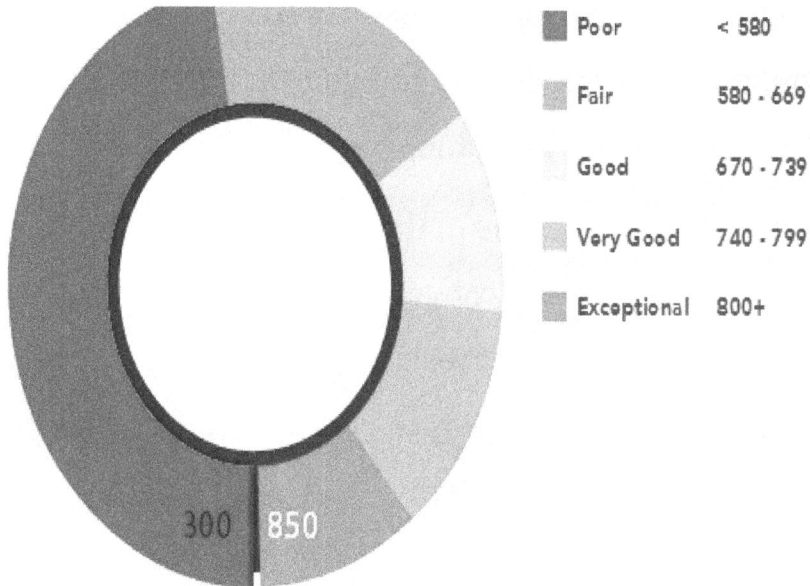

Poor	< 580
Fair	580 - 669
Good	670 - 739
Very Good	740 - 799
Exceptional	800+

For example, one lender may offer its lowest interest rates to people with FICO Scores above 730, while another lender only offers its lowest interest rates to people with FICO Scores above 760. A recent FICO study showed that consumers with lower recent credit activity generate a flatter (and thus weaker) score-odds rank-ordered relationship5. Similarly, Vantage Score reports that among the ~30–35 million consumers considered newly scoreable under Version 3.0 only ~3% had a score of above 680. Meanwhile, the estimated bad rate for all 35 million newly scoreable consumers is ~30%. There are therefore still thought to be many millions of potentially good borrowers in this newly scoreable sub-population around 25million but the new score is not yet strong enough to separate good and bad to the point that more than a few become lendable.

This is partly because of the inherent limitations of the data contained in credit bureau files and especially thin-files. Current credit bureau data are only part of the solution to increase access to credit-invisible consumers who are in fact credit-worthy, i.e., willing and able to pay back loans.

What's a FICO score?

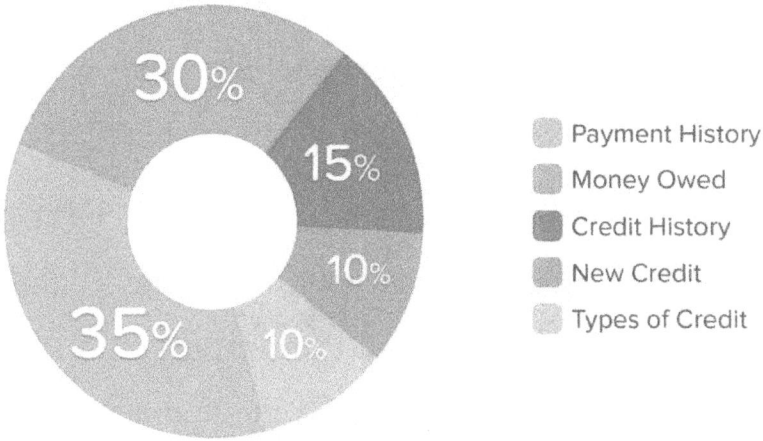

Although the exact formula for calculating the FICO score is secret, Fair Isaac (the developer of the FICO score) has disclosed the following components and the weight of their impact to the score:

Payment History –35%

Late payments on bills, such as a mortgage, credit card or automobile loan, will cause your FICO score to drop. The later Payments, and the longer they are past due (30, 60, 90 days), the more your score will suffer. Conversely, bills paid on time will improve your FICO score.

Amounts Owed Vs Credit Available – 30%

Keeping a low ratio of current revolving debt (such as credit card balances) to your total available revolving credit or credit limit will increase your score.

- For example, if you have a combined credit card limit of $10,000 and you have only $2,000 in balances – that's a credit utilization ratio of 20% and would be considered a good and reasonable ratio.

- By contrast, if you have a combined credit card limit of $10,000 and you have $9,500 in balances – that's a credit utilization ratio of 95%, and the score would be negatively impacted by it. The most obvious way to improve this aspect of your FICO score is by paying off debt and lowering your credit utilization ratio. Alternatively, receiving a credit limit increase may alsodrive down your utilization ratio (in the example shown above, if your limit were raised to $15,000 your utilization ratio would drop in both scenarios, demonstrating that you use revolving credit reasonably). Many experts believe a 20-30% credit utilization ratio is best. While opening new lines of credit may have a positive overall effect, opening too many have a negative impact.

The closing of existing revolving accounts will typically adversely affect this ratio and therefore have a negative impact on a FICO score. This is a common mistake that many people who are trying to improve their score make. Even worse, if it is an old account is closed, you will be reducing your length of credit.

Length of Credit – 15%

As your credit history ages, it can have a positive impact on your FICO score. A credit card that you have used reasonably for many years or a car loan that you've demonstrated on- time payments with for several years will make a positive impact. If all of your credit is newer, it is not seasoned enough to make a positive impact – since you haven't yet demonstrated a history of on-time payments and reasonable utilization. Your FICO score will likely increase as the average age of your credit increases.

New Credit – 10%

Hard credit inquiries, which occur when you apply for a credit card or loan (revolving or otherwise), can hurt your score, especially if done in great numbers; often three to five points per inquiry. If you're "rate shopping" for a mortgage or auto loan over a short period, you'll not likely experience a large decrease in your score as a result of these types of inquiries. Automated computer algorithms attempt to detect when your rate shopping (and not attempting to receive many new lines of credit), and they treat all of those hard inquiries as one. While all credit inquiries are recorded and displayed on your credit reports for two years, their impact decreases at the six-month and one-year mark, rendering them insignificant after a year.

Credit inquiries originated by you (such as pulling a credit report for personal use), an employer (for employee verification) or by companies initiating pre-screened offers of credit or insurance do not have any impact on a credit score. These are called "soft inquiries" or "soft pulls," and do not appear on a credit report used by lenders.

FICO Score Ranges

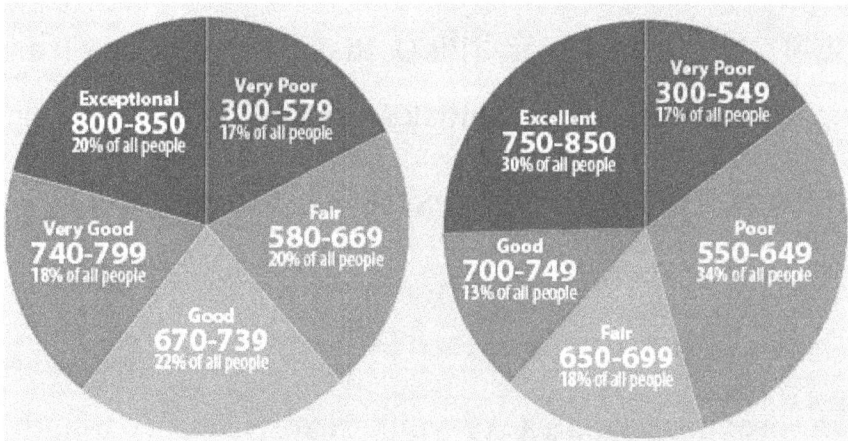

There are several types of FICO scores: generic, bankcard, personal finance, mortgage, installment loan, and auto. The generic or classic FICO score is between 300 and 850, and 37.2% of people had between 750 and 850 in 2012. According to FICO, the median FICO score in 2006 was 723, and 711 in 2011. The FICO bankcard score and FICO auto score are between 250 and 900. The FICO mortgage score is between 300 and 850. Higher scores indicate lower credit risk.

Each actually has 49 credit scores for the FICO scoring model because each of the three national credit bureaus, Equifax, Experian and the TransUnion has its own database. Data about an individual consumer can vary from bureau to bureau. FICO scores have different names at each of the different credit reporting agencies: Equifax (BEACON), TransUnion (FICO Risk Score, Classic) and Experian (Experian/FICO Risk Model.

Factors that determines a Fico score

1. Payment History

What is your track record?

Approximately 35% of your score is based on this category. The first thing any lender would want to know is whether you have paid past credit accounts on time. This is also one of the most important factors in a credit score.

Late payments are not an automatic "score-killer." An overall good credit picture can outweigh one or two instances of, say, late credit card payments. But having no late payments on your credit report doesn't mean you will get a "perfect score." Some 60%–65% of credit reports show no late payments at all. Your payment history is just one piece of information used in calculating your score.

Your score takes into account:

- Payment information on many types of accounts. These will include credit cards (such as Visa, MasterCard, American Express and Discover), retail accounts (credit from stores where you do business, such as department store credit cards), installment loans (loans where you make regular payments, such as car loans), finance company accounts and mortgage loans.

- Public record and collection items reports of events such as bankruptcies, foreclosures, suits, wage attachments, liens, and judgments. These are considered quite serious, although older items and items with small amounts will count less than more recent items or those with larger amounts. Bankruptcies will stay on your credit report for 7–10 years, depending on the type.

- Details on late or missed payments ("delinquencies") and public record and collection items. The score considers how late they were, how much was owed, how recently they occurred and how many there are. A 60-day late payment is not as risky as a 90-day late payment, in and of itself. But recency and frequency count too. A 60-day late payment made just a month ago will affect a score more than a 90-day late payment from five years ago.

- How many accounts show no late payments.
  A good track record on most of your credit accounts will increase your credit score.

2. Amounts Owed How much is too much?

Approximately 30% of your score is based on this category. Having credit accounts and owing money on them does not mean you are a high-risk borrower with a low score. However, owing a great deal of money on many accounts can indicate that a person is overextended, and is more likely to make some payments late or not at all.

Part of the science of scoring is determining how much is too much for a given credit profile.

Your score takes into account:

- The amount owed on all accounts.

Note that even if you pay off your credit cards in full every month, your credit report may show a balance on those cards. The total balance on your last statement is the amount that will show in your credit report.

- The amount owed on all accounts, and on different types of accounts. In addition to the overall amount you owe, the score considers the amount you owe on specific types of accounts, such as credit cards and installment loans.

- Whether you are showing a balance on certain types of accounts.

- In some cases, having a very small balance without missing a payment shows that you have managed credit responsibly, and may be slightly better than carrying no balance at all. On the other hand, closing unused credit accounts that show zero balances and that are in good standing will not raise your score.

- How many accounts have balances? A large number can indicate a higher risk of over-extension.

- How much of the total credit line is being used on credit cards and other "revolving credit" accounts? Someone closer to "maxing out" on many credit cards may have trouble making payments in the future.

- How much of installment loan accounts is still owed, compared with the original loan amounts?

- For example, if you borrowed $10,000 to buy a car and you have paid back $2,000, you owe (with interest) more than 80% of the original loan. Paying down installment loans is a good sign that you are able and willing to manage and repay debt.

3. Length of Credit History

How established is yours?

Approximately 15%of your score is based on this category. In general, a longer credit history will increase your score. However, even people who have not been using credit long may get high scores, depending on how the rest of the credit report looks.

Your score takes into account:

- How long your credit accounts have been established, in general. The score considers both the age of your oldest account and an average age of all your accounts.

- How long specific credit accounts have been established.

- How long it has been since you used certain accounts.

4. New Credit

Are you taking on more debt?

Approximately 10% of your score is based on this category. People tend to have more credit today and to shop for credit—via the Internet and other channels— more frequently than ever. Fair Isaac scores reflect this fact.

However, research shows that opening several credit accounts in a short period does represent greater risk— especially for people who do not have a long- established credit history. Multiple credit requests also represent greater credit risk. However, FICO scores do a good job of distinguishing between a search for many new credit accounts and rate shopping for one new account.

Your score takes into account:

- How many new accounts you have.

- The score looks at how many new accounts there are by type of account (for example, how many newly opened credit cards you have). It also may look at how many of your accounts are new accounts.

- How long it has been since you opened a new account. Again, the score looks at this by type of account.

- How many recent requests for credit you have made, as indicated by inquiries to the credit reporting agencies.

- Inquiries remain on your credit report for two years, although FICO scores only consider inquiries from the last 12 months.

- The length of time since the lender made the credit report inquiries.

- Whether you have a good recent credit history, following past payment problems. Re-establishing credit and making payments on time after a period of late payment behavior will help to raise a score over time.

5.   Types of Credit in Use

Is it a "healthy" mix? Approximately 10% of your score is based on this category.

The score will consider your mix of credit cards, retail accounts, installment loans, finance company accounts and mortgage loans. It is not necessary to have one of each, and it is not a good idea to open credit accounts you don't intend to use. The credit mix usually won't be a key factor in determining your score—but it will be more important if your credit report does not have a lot of other information on which to base a score.

Your score takes into account:

- What kinds of credit accounts you have, and how many of each.
- The score also looks at the total number of accounts you have. For different credit profiles, how many is too many will vary.

Secrets of the Credit Score

Score Secrecy

There are good reasons why credit scores are not secret anymore, nor are the foundational factors that comprise the score. By law, consumers have the right to see credit scores now. This report finds that except the credit score and a handful of other consumer scores, at this time, secrecy is the hallmark of many consumer scores. The factors that go into most scores are usually secret, the models used are usually secret, and in many cases, the score itself is also secret.

Score Accuracy

Because consumers do not have the right to correct or control what personal information goes into a consumer score as an attribute or factor, the accuracy of the scores is suspect. Consumers also do not have the right to see the scoring models used to make the score, nor do they typically have information about the model validity. Because of the lack of transparency, consumers cannot be assured of the reliability, fairness, or legality of scoring models. Inaccurate, incomplete, and illegal factors may be used today to make decisions about consumers without any oversight or redress.

How fast does score change?

Your score can change whenever your credit report changes. But your score probably won't change a lot from one month to the next. In a given three-month period, only about one in four people has a 20-point change in their credit score. While a bankruptcy or late payments can lower your score fast, improving your score takes time. That's why it's a good idea to check your score 6–12 months before applying for a big loan, so you have time to take action if needed. If you are actively working to improve your score, you'd want to check it quarterly or even monthly to review changes.

FICO Reveals How Common Credit Mistakes Affect Scores

DAMAGE POINTS: HOW MISTAKES AFFECT FICO SCORES		
Credit mistake	If your score is 680	If your score is 780
Maxed-out card	Down 10 to 30 pts.	Down 25 to 45 pts.
30-day late payment	Down 60 to 80 pts.	Down 90 to 110 pts.
Debt settlement	Down 45 to 65 pts.	Down 105 to 125 pts.
Foreclosure	Down 85 to 105 pts.	Down 140 to 160 pts.
Bankruptcy	Down 130 to 150 pts.	Down 220 to 240 pts.
Source: FICO		

Disclosed for the First Time, "Damage Points" Are Taken Off for Late Payments. Borrowers already knew that late payments hurt their credit scores, but for the first time, they now know the extent of that damage.

Did you max out your credit card? Expect a credit score drop of 10 to 45 points. Declare bankruptcy? Your score will plummet by up to 240 points, and your odds of getting credit will nose dive with it.

The "damage points" data, unveiled recently by Fair Isaac Corporation (FICO), a leading consumer credit-scoring system, are part of the most revealing glimpse into the firm's once-secret–and still mysterious–credit scoring model. The new information discloses how many points borrowers' scores will drop when they make the most common mistakes. "Help People Understand" Scores "I hope this information will help people to understand better FICO scores and the value for them of avoiding credit misstep," says FICO spokesman Craig Watts.

"It illustrates key points such as the higher your score, the farther it can fall if you stumble. Getting and maintaining a good score isn't complicated. We all just need to pay our bills on time, keep credit card balances low and take on new debt sparingly."

The greater transparency about FICO scores is important because of American consumers' ability to get credit rises and falls with the number. FICO, the company that pioneered credit scoring, assigns consumers a three-digit number from 300 to 850, depending on how well they handle credit. Other companies also offer scores, but FICO's version is the most widely used by lenders in determining whether a consumer can borrow and at what rate.

FICO's credit score has been around for decades, but only within the past decade have consumers gradually gained access to theirs. Though the raw numbers can be purchased, how they're figured remains a FICO secret, as closely guarded as the formula for Coca- Cola. Until recently, FICO revealed only broad categories of factors influencing the score, but not the number of points at stake for consumers who fail to pay as agreed.

Insurance Scores

Insurance scores, sometimes called credit-based insurance scores, fall under the FCRA.

The scores use credit scores and credit information to analyze prices for automobile insurance and home owner's insurance. Insurance scores differ from credit scores, and it appears that insurance companies may have their algorithms. More information about the use of credit scoring in insurance is available from the National Association of Insurance Commissioners and Consumer Reports.

Choice Trust, a Choice Point company, offers to sell home and auto insurance scores to individuals. FICO also has an insurance score product. A growing number of insurance carriers use custom scores that have been developed to meet that company's specific underwriting criteria.

Category Health Scores

Initial research for scoring done for this report found few health scores. Health scores are now in full circulation with little consumer awareness. The same questions raised above about transparency, secrecy factors, and use are relevant here. Other questions come into play as well. For example: can employers' purchase health scores?

Are health scores ever shared with debt collectors?

New health scoring systems that fall into the category of consumer scores will be developed and used shortly. It is also possible to foresee the development of family and neighborhood health scores based either a combination of traditional medical histories, genetic data, census data, data broker lists, environmental data, or histories of actual health treatments that may fall outside of HIPAA.

Health records held by health care providers or insurers are subject to the federal health privacy rules known as HIPAA.

While these records are available for many non-consensual uses, the information in the records should not normally be available to data brokers and score creators. However, the HIPAA rules do not cover health information held by gyms, websites, banks, credit card companies. Many health researchers, cosmetic medicine services, transit companies, fitness clubs, home testing laboratories, massage therapists, nutritional counselors, alternative medicine practitioners, disease advocacy groups, or marketers of non-prescription health products and foods. This vast class of largely unregulated health information is available as input to a health scoring algorithm.

Further, consumers routinely disclose health information to companies that promise to provide coupons. Consumers rarely understand that companies can collect personal information that they can later sell.

Personal health records (PHR) maintained by companies outside HIPAA protections may also become a source of unregulated health information for scoring.

Information disclosed through web searches or Internet browsing also typically remains unregulated by HIPAA, and all of the information can be evaluated for scoring.

Affordable Care Act Individual Health Risk Score.

Each in a health plan subject to risk adjustment under the Affordable Care Act (ACA) will be assigned a health risk score. This is a new score, and it is an important score especially because it is part of a federal program. In establishing the rules for health risk scores for individuals, the Health and Human Services Department effectively created a score that ultimately measures how sick a person is. The stated goal of the risk score is to create a relative measure of predicted health care costs for a particular enrollee. The scores are supposed to be phased out over the next four years.

The rules for the individual health risk score became official in March 2012, when the Department of Health and Human Services issued a final rule on reinsurance and risk adjustment under the Affordable Care Act.

The overall purpose of risk adjustment is to mitigate the impact of potential adverse selection and stabilize premiums in the individual and small group markets under the Affordable Insurance Exchanges that are part of the Affordable Care Act. A key element of the risk adjustment is the calculation of a plan's average actuarial risk so that the plan's average risk can be compared to other plans. The scores will be important because they will determine whether a plan pays or receives funds through the premium adjustment system. A plan might have an incentive to assign its insured a higher score. The use or disclosure of that score for another purpose could harm an individual.

Even disclosure of an honest score could be harmful. This is a new area and a new score, and there is much uncertainty about the use or misuse of the score. A plan's average risk is based on the risk score of each enrolled in that plan. An individual's health risk score will be a measure of how much that individual is likely to cost the health plan. The risk score measures likely health costs and is, in a very general way, a proxy for how sick an individual is.

How expensive an individual will be to ensure is important to insurers and employers, and the score can easily be misused. The HHS rule took some care to protect the privacy and security of an individual's risk score, including limits on the disclosure of identifiable elements when individual risk scores are passed on by a plan for use in State risk adjustment programs. Nevertheless, each in plans subject to risk adjustment will have his or her health risk score. The regulation is silent about individuals seeing their health risk score. If an insurer has a risk score for an individual, then it appears that it would be Protected Health Information as defined in the privacy rules issued under the rules of the Health Insurance Portability and Accountability Act (HIPAA). If that conclusion is correct, the score should be available to individuals under standard HIPAA rules. It is possible to foresee that an employer or lender or someone else with power over an individual might coerce the individual into obtaining his or her score and disclosing it.

Frailty Scores:

General Frailty Scores usually apply to the elderly. A good bit of research has been conducted using this score as a measure. As a result, a frailty score has become much more important in recent years. The research found that some frailty scores could predict mortality within one year.

Separate research indicated some frailty scores could usefully predict the likelihood of patient post-operative surgical complications or readmission to a hospital. While the scores can predict care needs, the scores can also be used to project costs simply, and this raises questions about possible misuse in non-health scores or marketing activities. Unless an HIPAA-covered entity calculates a frailty score using health records, the score is not likely covered by the HIPAA health privacy rules.

CMS Frailty Adjustment Score

The Canters for Medicaid developed a frailty score in the late 1990s. In 2004, after refinement, the CMS frailty measure was extended to more Medicare managed care organizations.

CMS is an HIPAA-covered entity so the score should be subject to the HIPAA health privacy rules. After CMS developed its score, several other models of frailty scores developed. Johns Hopkins University developed the Hopkins Frailty Score. Designed for use before surgery, the score would be calculated by a health care provider and would be subject to HIPAA. This predictive score in its original form has low factors compared to other scores and a small range. The factors are highly predictive, however, and this score is in widespread use.

It is unknown how many patients are assigned frailty scores, and it is unknown how many patients ever request their scores. Conceivably, a score held by a health care provider should be covered under HIPAA and patients should be able to request their score if one is there.

The concern with any predictive score, particularly a frailty score, is that it can escape into the hands of third parties where it can be used outside of the original intent of the score. The frailty score can be highly predictive, and therefore its use needs to be carefully guarded.

Personal Health Scores: WebMD, others

A personal health score is a growing category of scores that, at the moment, are relatively casual and aimed primarily at enhancing a consumer's self-understanding. These scores do not carry the same underwriting weight as, a large sample - set based, the formal statistical score would. The scores appear to be largely educational in nature, and voluntary.

Under the Affordable Care Act, wellness programs and health improvement are priorities. It is no surprise, then, that new health self-scoring activities for patient self-monitoring are coming online. These scores, by their nature, are typically generated by an online survey taken by the patient, with the resulting scores available to the patient. Although many variations exist of these sorts of more casual health scores, at this point most of the scores do not appear to be tied to benefit costs.

WebMD is a good exemplar of this kind of "personal" health score.

One Health Score is another exemplary. This score allows a consumer to rate their physical activity and its benefits. This score has a range of 1-100, with a score of 60 and above indicating that the person being scored has a basic level of physical activity. Professional athletes generally attain scores of 90 and over. These scores are likely not subject to HIPAA protections.

If the scores derived from information supplied by a consumer, then they have not protected health information under HIPAA unless an HIPAA covered entity calculated the score. A commercial website offering services to consumers is normally not an HIPAA covered entity. Even if the website maintains health records for the consumer, a use of the records is subject to the privacy policy and terms of service of the website.

Most consumers would likely not understand that health information held on their behalf by commercial websites has no legal privacy protections. How the use of these health scores will evolve and whether they will "escape" into the hands of marketers and data brokers is not known.

Complexity Scores

Complexity scores are beginning to spring up for various patient types and situations, for example, work to create a Complexity Score to Identify Hospitalized Patients at High Risk for Preventable Adverse Drug Events was founded in 2013. A complexity score used for treatment fall under HIPAA and does not qualify as a consumer score. A complexity score is used for marketing or to set rates may be a consumer score. This score is not a consumer score because it is for diagnostic use.

Peer to Peer Energy People Meter Score (EPM)

This score measures a residential customer's energy consumption and seeks to engage the customers in evaluating their energy consumption patterns. Consumer scores arising from Smart Grid or Internet usage is an emerging field. These scores are of great interest due to the approaching tsunami of information that connected devices in and out of the home, including cars, will provide. The EPM score is a proprietary score from Trove Data. The company has a range of analytics in the area of energy, not all of which qualify as consumer scores. The Energy People Meter score is of specific interest here.

Youth Delinquency Scores

The Foundation for Information Policy Research in the United Kingdom completed a report identifying the growth in children's databases and assessing the data protection and privacy implications.

The report describes structured assessment tools for the youth justice system in England and Wales that create profiles of young offenders by examining the factors that may have brought each youth into contact with the criminal justice system. The assessments are scored for adverse factors, and the score is used to predict the likelihood of re- offending. Whether any comparable U.S. scoring systems exist is unknown.

Predictive Anti---Fraud Scores:

US Postal Service Office of Inspector General. The US Postal Service Office of Inspector General has a predictive analytics team that uses predictive fraud scores to address point-of- sale fraud issues. As described, the

Postal Service has a customized fraud detection tool. "Using more than 30 indicators to search a wide variety of data, the fraud detection tool flags and ranks instances of suspicious.

activity, allowing investigators in the Postal Service's Office of the Inspector General to decide which leads to pursue.

ENVIRONMENTAL SCORES

EPA Health Risk Score

The EPA uses substantial predictive analytics tools and has a Human Toxicity Risk Score that can be computed in aggregate, by neighbourhood/per square mile.

In a groundbreaking series of articles in 2005, the Associated Press used the EPA data to map the air quality risk scores for every neighbourhood in the U.S. The AP mapped the EPA toxicity risk scores to socio-economic and racial factors for each neighbourhood from the 2000 Census to determine the makeup of who was breathing the dirtiest air in America. The headlines across the country read, in some variation, that minorities suffer most from industrial pollution.

The results established important understandings about neighbourhoods and toxicity, and the resulting snapshot of where and how factory pollution was impacting neighbourhoods and people were deservedly much- discussed. These results are examples of beneficial uses of scores and what today would be called large datasets or "big data.

How the formerly secret credit score became available to the public.

Scores were unknown to most consumers through the 50s, 60s, 70s, and 80s. Trickles of a score that was that could be used to deny a person credit but which was not revealed to consumers began to leak out slowly to some policymakers, particularly around the time ECOA passed. But scores had not entered the minds of most people.

In May 1990, the Federal Trade Commission wrote commentary indicating that risk scores (credit scores) did not have to be made available to consumers. But when scoring began to be used for mortgage lending in the mid-90s, many consumers finally began hearing about a credit score, most for the first time, and most when they were being turned down for a loan.

A slow roar over the secrecy and opacity of the credit score began to build. By the late 90s, the secrecy of credit scores and the fact that people could not see the underlying methodology or factors that went into the score or the range of the score to determine how the number should be interpreted was a full-blown policy issue.

Beginning in 2000, events pushing toward increased credit score disclosure began to escalate, culminating in a rapid-fire series of events that eventually dismantled credit score secrecy and non-disclosure.

It is fair to say that a good deal of the escalation of events began when E-Loan, an Internet lender, took the extraordinary step of making credit scores public in February 2000 via a website according to research. The scores were free, and the word got out quickly to consumers.

In one month, the site attracted more than 25,000 customers and a lot of attention. The website was shut down after six weeks; Fair Isaac, at that time, had a rule prohibiting the disclosure of FICO scores to consumers unless they were turned down for a loan. But although the site was being shut down, consumer appetite for their scores had been whetted. This incident was a tipping point due to how it popularized the score issue among consumers.

Ongoing disclosure challenges and other issues with consumer credit scores

During the FACTA process, a growing trend was captured via the public comment process, that is, that the use of credit scores was greatly expanding to other areas of business. One area of concern was the use of credit scores to determine homeowner and auto insurance rates. Some individuals who had good driving records, for example, all of a sudden, upon renewal, were receiving much higher insurance rates due to a weak credit score. This practice has been the subject of much discussion, study, consternation, and some law making, with varying results.

During this general period that FACTA was being debated, the crime of identity theft began to become known and understood.

New laws regarding the setting of insurance rates by a credit score impacted by identity fraud have been percolating through the states now as a result.

Disclosure of credit scores in now a non-issue. But while credit scores have been made public, it is not so with all other consumer scores. Consumers who want to see their identity score, their Z score, or many other scores cannot. Consumers who inquire about scores, or even the existence of a possible score, are not always told whether or not a score is being used. Similar if not identical arguments are used today to keep some consumer scores secret as were used to keep the credit score secret. While the credit score and its use, has been regulated by FACTA and now also by Basel II, this is not so for the broadening range of consumer scores that are increasingly attaching themselves to consumers.

The heightened availability and almost complete lack of oversight and regulation of the newer consumer scores combined with almost complete opacity regarding consumer scores' (minus credit and some forms of insurance scores) models, factors, ranges, validation, bias, sample size, and so forth has created a swath of non-disclosure and secrecy that consumers are at this point largely unaware of.

Richard Berk Algorithm

Criminologist Richard Berk developed a predictive model to identify murderers. Kim Zetter of Wired wrote, "To create the software, researchers assembled a dataset of more than 60,000 crimes, including homicides, then wrote an algorithm to find the people behind the crimes who were more likely to commit murder when paroled or put on probation." Pennsylvania, Maryland, and Washington D.C. use the software.

The algorithm, Inc.

Consumer scores generated by sophisticated mathematical models that detect patterns in information are often predictive, involve one or more algorithms, and rely on factors that describe individuals in some way.

The historical databases and raw consumer information that supply information to a scoring model can be both wide and large. Credit scoring databases used to build score models, for example, may contain records of well over 100,000 individuals, and the model may measure over 100 factors or variables.

Behavioural scoring databases that store transactional data on, for example, retail or other purchases, repayment, or other activities can be even larger.

Additional secrets of credit scoring revealed.

That same month, on February 22, 2000, California Senator Liz Figueroa introduced SB 1607 which would give Californians access to their credit scores. Specifically, the bill required lenders to give customers a copy of the credit score obtained to solicit a loan or accept a loan application.

Bowing to the growing pressure, Fair Isaac began to releases some information about the factors that were used in its credit scoring model, FICO, in June 2000, but they did not release the actual score at that time. One of the arguments they made was that too much disclosure would allow manipulation of the score. Governor Grey Davis signed the credit score disclosure legislation in September 2000, and the law took effect July 1, 2001.

An uncomfortable situation arose for federal lawmakers: Californians were the only ones who had access to their credit score. It was a classic recipe for national legislation on credit score disclosure.

In 2002, the FTC reversed its 1990 decision and concluded that consumers should be able to see their credit scores. As of December 2004, the Fair Credit Reporting Act as modified by the Fair and Accurate Credit Transactions Act, or FACTA, ended score secrecy formally and required consumer reporting agencies to provide consumers with more extensive credit score information, upon request.

Also made available to the public was the context of the score (its numeric range), the date the score was created, some of the key factors that adversely affected the score.

The Federal Trade Commission is required by FACTA to study various aspects of credit scoring, insurance scoring, disparities, modelling, and more. Much remains unknown about scoring models, even those that fall under FACTA such as credit scoring models. The formulas, which are important in verifying many aspects of the scoring model, are still secret.

Credit Basics

Credit is an arrangement you make with a company or individual to receive goods, products, or services now that you will pay later. It's a measure of your financial reliability and can be used for small or large purchases. Loans, which are often credit-based, involve borrowed money that you have to pay back — often with interest. Credit is offered in many forms, such as:

Revolving credit

When you get a credit card, you're offered funds that you can continually use, up to your established limit, as you pay down the balance. Interest accrues (grows) on the money you borrow until you pay it back.

Installments or term loans:

As with student and automobile loans, an instalment loan is one that is paid back over time with a set number of scheduled payments. You don't get additional credit as you pay down the loan. And keep in mind that, regardless of whether you graduate from school or not, student loans must be paid back with interest.

Mortgage

When you need a home loan, you take out a mortgage. The loan is secured by the property you're purchasing (collateral).

What is data aggregation?

Alternative data refers to the inclusion of non-financial payment reporting data in credit files, such as telecom and energy utility payment.

Types of alternative data:

Alternative data in the broadest sense refers to any non- financial information that can be used to estimate the lending risk of an individual. Information includes:

- Utility bills (such as electricity, gas, and heating oil)
- Telecommunications bills (such as landlines and mobile telephones)
- Rental payments
- Electronic payments (remittances, withdrawals, transfers, etc.)

United States

In the United States, credit files include negative information, such as delinquencies as well as positive information, such as repayment of debts. Still, an estimated 35 to 54 million Americans have insufficient credit information to qualify for the mainstream credit. If immigrants in the United States are included, that number exceeds 70 million. Access to credit is thus a Catch-22 for many poor Americans—one needs credit to get credit. Research suggests that the inclusion of alternative data in credit files could bring many of these individuals into the credit fold. That is, non-financial positive payment information, such as rents or utility payments, may give credit agencies enough information to rate previously unscorable individuals known as the unbanked. These newly scored individuals have risk profiles similar to those already in the mainstream credit system. Racial minorities, women, and the poor disproportionally benefit. Furthermore, loans become smarter. Including alternative data has little effect on the credit mainstream, those already scorable in the current system.

Furthermore, this increase in data decreases the number of bad loans.

Experian purchased Rent Bureau in June 2010, which houses rental payment histories on over 7 million US residents, this data will now be included in consumer credit reports as of January 2011. This will benefit those that overlap with the 50 million US underbanked consumers. The danger with this is that it will provide a further variable to damage credit scores of those that do not, for example, manage their rental payments on time in addition to their other credit arrangements.

Current use of alternative data:

Since the financial crisis of late 2008, many Americans have struggled with the negative change to their credit score. Reduced credit lines resulting in a new group of consumers in need of liquidity forced this growing consumer segment to seek alternative financial services providers. Businesses relying on traditional credit reports to make credit decisions have had limited to no visibility on the new credit usage behaviours of this growing portion because alternative data is not information that the traditional bureaus capture or tend to report.

Utilities and telecoms firms in several states have started reporting their data to CRAs. PRBC, a consumer credit reporting agency based in Kennesaw, Georgia, allows consumers to self-enrol and build a positive credit file based on their timely payments for bills such as rent, utilities, cable, telephone, and insurance that are not automatically reported to the other bureaus. TransUnion, First American CredCo, and LexisNexis have all recently released products involving alternative data.

Concerns about the use of alternative data in credit files

Some concerns about the use of alternative data have been raised over the long-term consequences of fully reporting utility and telecom payments to credit rating agencies. There are concerns that state and local incentives to not pay bills on time (for example, some states provide heating oil subsidies if payments are missed) may cause deterioration in credit scores over time. There is also concern that people who open accounts with only alternative data will become over- extended. Recent research shows, however, that the inclusion of alternative data does not degrade credit scores over a one-year period.

Alternative Data for Credit Around the World

(aka Wealth Score Metric)

Recently, the World Bank issued a global credit information sharing standard that included a section on alternative data. The World Bank steadfastly endorses the use of fully reported non-financial payment data in credit origination processes and considers it a powerful tool for driving financial inclusion in emerging markets. More recently, in the Financial Inclusion 2020 Roadmap, Accion highlighted the great value of alternative data as an instrument to increase financial inclusion and help achieve their FI2020 objectives.

In low-income nations, alternative data is often the only type of data available for credit scoring. The population is often not formally employed, lacks a credit history, cannot fulfil loan application requirements, and has insufficient capital. Even when these requirements are fulfilled, lending institutions often have very little experience with clients' economic activity leading to untailored loan products.

Electronically-available alternative data, such as bill payments, mobile telephone bills, rental payments, and electronic transaction data, could be used to score these individuals and enter millions in low-income countries into a more modern credit ratings system.

Can scoring rental vastly improve Credit Access

There has been much discussion and several studies over the years regarding the potential value of leveraging rental data in assessing consumer credit risk. Which raises the question: Should rental data be widely reported to the three primary consumer credit reporting agencies (CRAs)?

If rental data was reported, this might mean some consumers without loans or credit cards would get a FICO® Score, and gain access to more affordable credit. But how many? And how many of these consumers would be considered creditworthy by prospective lenders?

In 2015, FICO introduced FICO Score 9, which scores rental data. This coincided with the first evidence of sufficient positive and negative rental data at the CRAs, a necessary condition for adding this data into the FICO Score algorithm.

Not Enough Rental Data in Credit Bureau Files Today

Much like with utility and telcom data (covered in a prior Truth Squad blog, rental data is quite rarely encountered in consumer credit files.

The US Census Bureau estimates that there are 240 million adults in the US, with 35% living in rental housing.

Of the roughly 80 million US adults who live in rental housing, we found that just 270,000 (or 0.3%) of those consumers have a rental trade line reported in their credit file.

In fact, rental data makes up less than 1% of all the credit data being reported to the credit bureaus.

So while some have claimed that the inclusion in a credit bureau risk score calculation of rental data currently reported to the CRAs would significantly move the needle as far as scorable rates or access to credit, it's just not the case.

Our research showed that only ~5,000 total consumers (out of 200+ million scorable files) became FICO scorable as a result of the inclusion of rental data currently found in their credit file. In the context of mortgage lending, a mere 1,795 consumers had scores that met the accepted FICO Score cut- off of 620 or greater once rental data was included in their score calculation.

Does Rental Data Make Thin Files Fatter?

Most mortgage lenders and the Government Sponsored Enterprises (GSEs) have underwriting standards that require a consumer to demonstrate experience in making payments on more than one trade line — typically two to three trade lines. So perhaps the value of rental data is that it would allow more people to meet these criteria?

We checked how many consumers have a FICO® Score above 620, and have two or three trade lines reported to the CRA where one of those trade lines is rent. There were

280 people with two trade lines, one being rent, and 110 people with three trade lines, one being rent. That's great news for these

390 individuals, but it shows that rental data currently reported to the CRA does not have a significant impact on access to credit.

Fact: The reporting of rental data has not reached meaningful volume such that inclusion of this data presently has a material impact on the total number of scorable US consumers or access to credit.

How do we get more rental data to score?

Rental data does have potential to improve credit access, but not until much more of it is reported to credit bureaus. So why do we see so little rental data being reported?

The challenges of achieving broad national scale in rental reporting are significant. The first is the disaggregation of the furnisher market — much of the rental market is single property landlords. The second is a regulatory compliance hurdle — there is a general aversion among potential furnishers to take on the operational and compliance risks posed by becoming a CRA data furnisher.

We would encourage policy makers to support the broader inclusion of rental data at the CRAs to support consumers' access to affordable credit. Should rental data start to flow into the credit report in meaningful volumes, the FICO®

Score 9 algorithm can reward consumers for their successful history of on-time rental payments.

In the meantime, scores like FICO® Score XD — which analyzes non-traditional credit data found outside of the credit report — provide an onramp to mainstream credit for people with limited credit experience.

2.   Does Vantage Score Use Alternative Data?

In the era of Big Data, so-called alternative data holds a special promise — to shine a new light on consumer behavior. When it comes to credit scoring, alternative data means data not being used today for risk assessment, and specifically, data not found in the credit bureaus. Lenders hope to score this data could allow them to make

faster, better decisions on people who don't have FICO®
Scores — the "unscorable" with sparse or no credit
bureau data on file.

Hoping to jump on the alt-data bandwagon, the three
main US credit reporting agencies – through their Vantage
Score business have been claiming that their score uses
alternative data to score more consumers than the
industry-leading FICO® Score. It sounds good, but is it
true?

Claim: Vantage Score leverages alternative data to
score millions of more consumers than FICO Scores.

Truth: The "alternative" data Vantage Score uses
utilities and cell phone bills — as reported to the credit
bureaus. The FICO Score also uses the same data.
Moreover, the vast majority of utility and cell phone bill
data is NOT reported to the credit bureaus, and so is NOT
used by Vantage Score.

The fact is that Vantage Score, like the FICO Score,
doesn't analyse any data that isn't at the credit bureaus.
By definition, that means it doesn't score any alternative
data whatsoever.

Nor is scoring utility payments and cell phone payments new. The FICO Score has been doing it since day one, in 1989.

What makes this claim even more misleading is that non-loan payments such as utility payments and cell phone bills CAN help score more people. That's because the vast majority of this data is not reported to the credit bureaus. Only a tiny portion of it is included in the credit bureau data.

How sparsely reported is this information? An estimated 92% of US adults have a cell phone — think about it, everyone you know does. However, just 2.5% (or roughly 7 million) of all consumer credit bureau files contain telco account information.

The story is similar on the utility account side, where over 60% of American adults pay for utilities, but just 2.4% of consumer credit bureau files contain utility (non-telco) payment information. Judging by credit bureau data alone — the data Vantage Score accesses — you would think most Americans don't have water or electricity in their homes.

As for the notion that using this data can score more people, here's another fact: Of the unscorable population that have sparse data at the credit bureaus, less than 2% have any telco or utility data.

Now, where is Americans' data on utility and phone payments? And how can we score it?

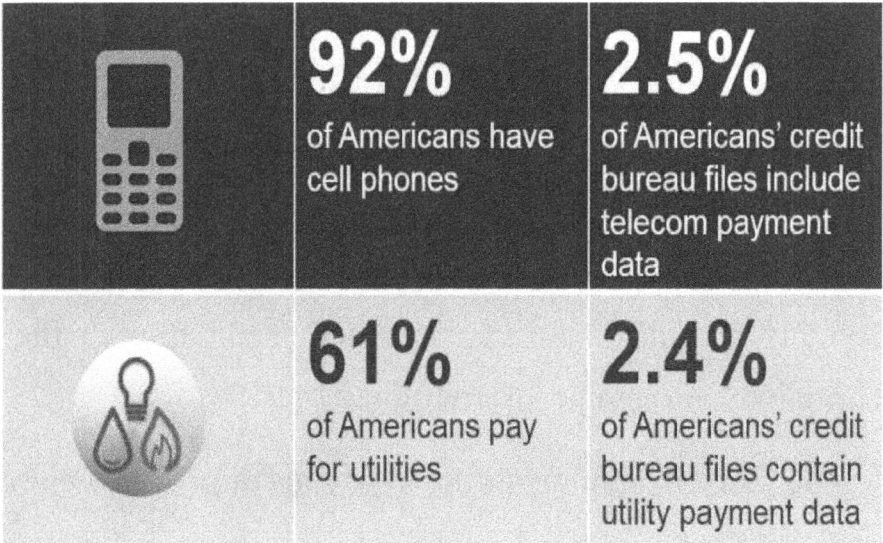

📱	**92%** of Americans have cell phones	**2.5%** of Americans' credit bureau files include telecom payment data
💡	**61%** of Americans pay for utilities	**2.4%** of Americans' credit bureau files contain utility payment data

This data is reported to other databases, which contain payment information on more than 200 million unique consumers. FICO® Score XD uses this data, FICO's next-generation credit score meant to increase the scorable universe through the use of (truly) alternative data.

There simply isn't an opportunity to safely and soundly score millions of more Americans using credit bureau data alone. The FICO Score has fully mined the value found in that data for assessing risk. To score more people, we need to use truly alternative data — i.e., data not found at the credit bureaus. It's perhaps not surprising that the three credit bureaus that own Vantage Score want to stick to the data they own, but to call any of this data "alternative" is absurd.

3. Can Looser Scoring Standards Help Millions of More Americans Get Mortgages?

Access to credit and the path to homeownership are important parts of the American way of life. That's why it's critical to understand what can be done to improve financial inclusion and what won't work.

For months now, the three main US consumer reporting agencies through their Vantage Score business have been claiming that millions of credit-starved Americans can get access to mortgages through the "innovation" of simply eliminating long-standing and essential minimum credit scoring criteria. This isn't innovation, and it won't help borrowers. It's time to set the record straight.

Claim: By loosening the minimum scoring criteria, Vantage Score can give millions of currently unscorable Americans a credit score, making them mortgage-ready.

Truth: Scoring sparse and old data may give more Americans a score, but it won't help those Americans who are seeking homeownership credit. Even worse, it locks millions of Americans into unfairly low scores.

To begin, let's look at why some people don't have FICO® Scores. The answer is that there are FICO® Score minimum scoring criteria, which play a critical role in ensuring the robustness and accuracy of our credit scoring system, and by extension the soundness of lending decisions based on that system.

The so-called "unscorable" are people who don't meet these minimum criteria, for one of four reasons:

The question is, if we were to loosen the FICO Score's minimum scoring criteria, how many consumers would score 620 (a common lending threshold) or higher? And how many of those consumers would be in the market for a mortgage?

Segment	Size	Median Age	Why Can't They Be Scored?	Typical Credit Application Rate
Credit Retired	~7M	71	Only old account data on file — median time since last account update is 4.5 years	1 – 4%
Credit Impaired	~18M	43	Only old account data on file — median time since last account update is 34 months	20 – 30%
New to Credit	~3M	24	Less than 6 months of credit history – not enough to accurately rate risk	35 – 40%
No Traditional Credit File	~25M	25	No data at the credit bureau	35 – 40%

To find out, we developed a research score that, like Vantage Score, eliminates most of the time-tested FICO Score minimum scoring criteria. As a result, it can assign a score for the people with sparse credit files who are currently FICO unscorable. We aligned this score to the same 300-850 score range used by the FICO Score.

As shown in Figure 1, the largest of the unscorable segments is about 25 million people who have No Traditional Credit File whatsoever, and are therefore unreachable by any credit bureau score. Our research score couldn't score these people, and neither could any other credit bureau score.

Credit Retired: consumers with no recently active/updated accounts and no historical signs of payment blemishes. These consumers skew older (median age = 71), and have voluntarily walked away from the use of credit accounts – they've paid it all back. Unsurprisingly, their appetite for new credit is extremely low; fewer than 5% of the Retired Credit population recently applied for credit.

Credit Impaired: consumers with no recently active/updated accounts, and with historical signs of serious delinquency or other negative behavior on file (e.g., collections, public records). This segment comprises almost two-thirds of all unscorable accounts on file at the credit bureaus, and in many cases captures consumers who had a negative event and subsequently lost access to credit. As such, their traditional credit file is "frozen" at the consumer's moment of financial distress. These consumers tend to be middle-aged (median age = 43) and show moderate interest in new credit (20-30% recently applied for credit).

New to Credit: consumers with 1+ recently active/updated accounts, but with less than 6 months of credit history. These consumers skew young (median age = 24), and a typical borrower in this segment has recently opened their first credit card with a very low (<$1,000) credit limit. They are relatively credited hungry, with some 40% of this segment having recently applied for additional credit.

When we look at the research score distribution for these segments, something interesting emerges.

People with higher scores are largely people in the Credit Retired category people who aren't looking for credit. When we look at the research score.

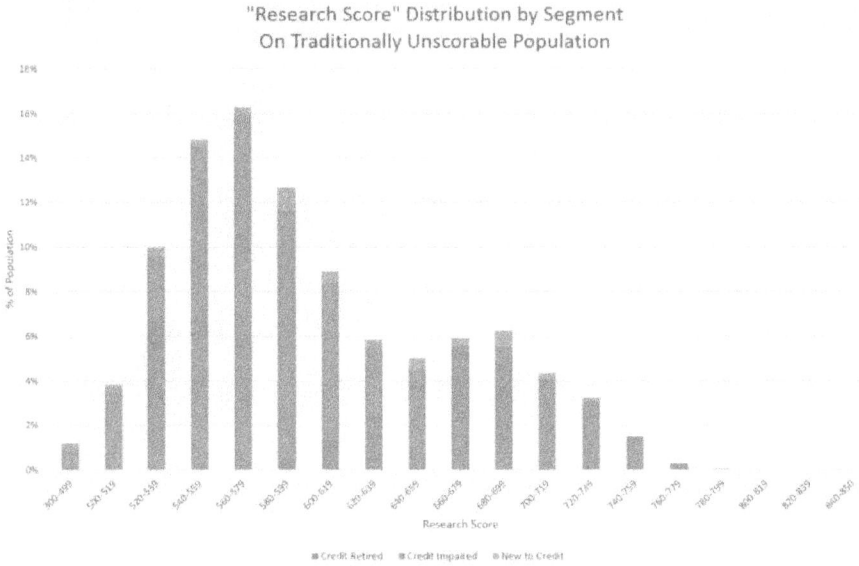

"Research Score" Distribution by Segment
On Traditionally Unscorable Population

As a group, all the unscorable people together score lower than the traditionally scorable cohort: The median score on this unscorable population is 585, roughly 130 points lower than the median FICO score of 715. Only about 33% of this research population score 620 or higher, and the vast majority of those (80%) hail from the Credit Retired segment. If we focus on a score threshold of 680 or above, that figure jumps to almost 95%!

Additionally, note the strong downward skew to the score distribution. The majority of the more than 18M consumers in our Credit Impaired segment — the people who had a negative financial event and either lost or never had access to traditional credit — would receive a score too low to qualify for the credit.

Even worse, because the Credit Impaired consumers lost all access to credit, they have no payment or account balance changes being reported to the consumer reporting agencies. Therefore, these consumers have no way to demonstrate their return to credit-worthiness. Many of these people have overcome, persevered, and recovered, and their recovery is not reflected in their frozen credit bureau file. Every fairly constructed credit scoring approach must give people the ability to demonstrate their return to creditworthiness – FICO's approach to scoring more consumers using alternative data does, Vantage Score's approach does not.

What does this show us? Despite claims by Vantage Score, weakening the minimum scoring criteria will not empower millions of low-risk mortgage credit seekers.

As articulated by the FICO white paper Can Alternative Data Expand Credit Access? The responsible approach to scoring more consumers is to enhance sparse traditional credit files with rich data sources such as payment history on cable and telco accounts — data that is very rarely found in credit bureau records. This approach will help consumers on their financial journey into mainstream lending.

4. Latest Ways to Score Risk Can Improve Financial Inclusion.

The path to a better lifestyle includes access to credit. Unfortunately, an estimated 3 billion people worldwide fall outside the credit mainstream – they either don't have a bank account or they have so little data at the credit bureau that lenders may skip over them, or classify them as very high risk.

That's why FICO has announced the FICO Financial Inclusion Initiative, a global effort to increase access to affordable credit for consumers and businesses with limited or no credit history. We're using a combination of business partnerships, innovative new products, mobile platforms and cloud-based services to help credit grantors make affordable credit more accessible to unbanked and underbanked adults worldwide.

5. Latest CRA Guidance Promotes Use of Alternative Data (aka Wealth Score Metric) in Lending

The potential of alternative data in consumer lending decisions continues to be a hot topic in Washington, D.C., with the latest evidence seen in developments related to the Community Reinvestment Act (CRA). When federal banking agencies recently revised their Q&As for CRA compliance, their focus on the use of alternative data caught my eye. This development is welcome news for those here at FICO and our many existing and prospective customers.

Adopted in 1977, the CRA is intended to encourage depository institutions to help meet the credit needs of the communities in which they operate, including low- and moderate-income neighbourhoods. The Act requires federal banking agencies (the OCC, FDIC and Federal Reserve – "Agencies") to conduct periodic reviews of each depository institution's efforts in this area. CRA regulations provide various methods of evaluating bank performance, corresponding to differences in institutions' asset sizes, structures and operations. After a thorough assessment of the institution, bank examiners assign a CRA rating and issue a public performance evaluation.

CRA regulations allow a financial institution's lending performance to be evaluated, in part, by the institution's "use of innovative or flexible lending practices safely and soundly to address the credit needs of low- or moderate-income individuals or geographies." Notably, the latest version of the Q&A guidance includes a new clarification of this standard involving the use of alternative credit histories in mortgage and consumer lending programs. The Agencies discuss the use of alternative data, such as rent and utility payments, "to evaluate low- or moderate-income individuals who lack sufficient conventional credit histories and who would be denied credit under the institution's traditional underwriting standards." The Agencies consider this use of alternative credit histories as an "innovative or flexible lending practice" that enhances the "success and effectiveness" of the institution's lending program.

This revised CRA guidance gives financial institutions an additional reason to adopt scoring innovations that leverage alternative data responsibly to expand credit access for communities with low- or moderate-income consumers.

Responsibly expanding credit access has always been a central focus at FICO. This April, FICO and our partners, LexisNexis® and Equifax®, announced the availability of an alternative data score, FICO® Score XD. This score leverages data found outside the traditional credit file to identify creditworthy individuals among the 50+ million unscorable consumers in the US. FICO® Score XD considers alternative data such as cable, landline, mobile and utility payments, along with select public record information.

FICO® Score XD is being piloted by many of the largest lenders for use in bankcard and other unsecured lending programs, and we have plans to expand it to additional loan types. FICO research shows that the score can serve as an on- ramp to the mainstream credit market for people who otherwise might have great difficulty in obtaining credit.

My colleague has written a series of blog posts detailing our research and the promise that this new score holds.

We're excited about the results we've seen so far – and to see like- minded enthusiasm from regulators and policy makers about the emerging potential of alternative data in lending.

6. Why "Alternative Data" Is not an Alternative in sense

In the last few weeks, I have been asked on several occasions to comment on the use of "alternative data" in credit scoring and risk assessment. Sometimes it seems I am being asked to defend using "traditional data" rather than the new, cool stuff.

I'm going to share a few observations that I hope can put this in context. Here's the first: There is value in what people call "alternative data." It just isn't alternative.

People often talk about alternative data as if it is somehow magical and, to paraphrase a famous UK lager ad, able to reach places traditional data can't. It reminds me of how fans talked about "alternative rock" bands like The Sex Pistols or Nirvana — they were just cooler than "classic rock" bands like The Rolling Stones.

How often have you seen words like limited, narrow and restricted used to describe traditional data, and terms like broader, voluminous and diverse to describe alternative data? Very often these people fail to refer to the value of the data. And that's what counts.

Who cares if I "only" have your credit card payments and deposit history, if the value of this data far outweighs that of any other data I can get? When you have a person's credit history, the law of diminishing returns for other data sources sets in pretty early on.

That's why I say alternative data isn't an alternative. It's additional. ("Additional data" doesn't sound so cool, does it?) It's a false choice to imply otherwise because no lender is going to throw away analysis of a consumer's payment history.

For example, in a recent project building a scoring model outside the US, we found that the "alternative" data added 8% relative to the ROC, a measure of a predictive model's power. Now, 8% is non-trivial and certainly worth having, but it's not even double-digits. Would you abandon the 92% of the predictive power the traditional data provide? Of course not.

Sometimes we need additional data because the traditional stuff is missing completely, too short or too old. Done right, the use of such data is in all our interests. I'll write more about what "done right" means in a future post. In the meantime, remember – "alternative data" for lending isn't.

ALTERNATIVE DATA AND THE UNBANKED

Alternative data' can improve access to credit for millions of Americans. It can do this by overcoming two important limitations of today's best practices in lending, which rely heavily on credit scores from the three major credit reporting agencies. The two principal limitations of current best practices are that:

- Many consumers remain 'credit invisible', meaning that no credit scores are available for them.
- The accuracy of scores today, while very good, is still sufficiently limited that many potentially.

Good borrowers must necessarily be denied access to credit because they cannot be statistically separated from poorer risks Alternative data show significant potential to improve the status quo by enhancing the accuracy of existing scores (achieving better risk separation), and by rendering visible many of today's credit invisible. Progress will come about through the private sector efforts of established lenders and credit bureaus, as well as the innovations of FinTechs, alternative data vendors and big data analytics firms, operating in the free market. There may also be a limited role for regulatory and legislative initiatives. The result will be better and fairer access to credit for individuals, with macro benefits for the whole economy.

Consumers in the United States are heavy users of credit. Consumer debt, including personal loans, secured real-estate loans, auto loans, credit cards, and student loans, total over

$12 trillion. Even excluding mortgages, this amounts to over

$30,000 of debt per household1. Access to credit is an important and widespread benefit because it allows consumers to purchase productive assets such as a car, pickup truck or work tools, to accelerate consumption from future earnings, invest in education for future earning power, enjoy tax advantages (through a home mortgage), or to build wealth, among other opportunities.

On the other hand, because consumer lending relies heavily on the use of credit scores, millions of Americans currently do not have beneficial access to credit either because their credit score is too low or because they have no credit score at all.

The people who have no credit score are sometimes referred to as 'credit invisible'; there are two ways in which they may come to have no score:

- They have no credit file at any of the three major credit bureaus—such people are referred to in the trade as 'no hits.'

- Despite having a credit file, there is insufficient recent information in that file to produce a score—these people are referred to as 'thin-files

Exhibit 1 is a schematic that shows all US adults classified as either 'scoreable', thin-file or no-hit.

The scoreable population is further separated into those with higher scores ('lendable') or lower scores ('not lendable'). Different lenders set different boundaries between lendable and not lendable; here the proportions are consistent with a FICO score or Vantage Score of 680 as the approximate dividing line. There are several underlying reasons why the no-hits and thin files may be credit-invisible, including:

- They never used credit: for example, students, recent legal (or undocumented) immigrants, or millennials seeking credit for the first time may all have zero recorded credit history.
- They no longer use credit: for example, older people may have paid off all debt, or avoided using credit; some people are cash-rich and do not

require credit; others may have lost access to credit due to previous economic difficulties.

- They have made very limited use of credit.

The invisible credit population is varied and contains a high proportion of minorities.

The Financial Industry Regulatory Authority estimates that only 51% of African-Americans and 58% of Latinos have a credit score, compared to the 75% of all American adults who have a credit score2. Lacking access to mainstream credit, credit invisible is vulnerable to high-priced credit such as payday loans, buy-here-pay-here auto loans, lease-to-own, and other 'informal' high-rate lending products. If they can access credit at all, it is expensive for them to borrow short- term and almost impossible to obtain a mortgage to buy a home.

For a subset of the invisible credit population, as well as many of the low-score/non-lendable, of course, 'access to credit' would mean getting into debt and might not necessarily be a good thing, for either the borrower or the lender. While we should encourage qualified access to credit, we should not regard 'credit to everyone' as a correct policy goal. One of the few undisputed errors leading up to the financial crisis was the appeal to "roll the dice a little bit more" with respect to subsidized home-ownership. The proper goal is sure to make credit available at a fair price to those who are most likely to benefit from the loans and also repay them. Interestingly, there is evidence to suggest that quite a high percentage of the credit invisible could meet these requirements.

A CLOSER LOOK AT LENDING AND CREDIT SCORES

In recent decades, consumer lending has moved towards the practice of making lending decisions guided by statistical models. Lenders evaluate potential borrowers through an underwriting process that relies heavily on credit scores derived from data in applicants' credit files. These credit files are maintained by the major credit bureaus (Experian, Equifax and the TransUnion). In effect, a credit score provides a lender with a guide to the probability of being repaid, in the event, they decide to approve a loan application.

Despite their widespread adoption, there are some limitations to credit scores and many aspects of their creation and use that are not widely understood. We have included a brief explanatory section later in this article which may be useful to anyone unfamiliar with credit scores, or for those needing a refresher. One point we will make here, however, is that credit scores, though enormously helpful, are still far from perfect.

Let's take it as given that consumer scores provide a reasonably accurate rank-ordering of relative credit risk among potential borrowers for whom such scores are available. Lenders primarily use scores to determine whether or not they will lend to a given borrower; they typically set a score below which they will generally not lend, often referred to as a 'cut-off score'. Scores are also used to help set the terms of a loan, like a loan (or line) amount and the interest rate. Applicants with higher credit scores are less likely to default and can, therefore, secure larger loan amounts and typically are asked to pay lower interest rates.

A credit score, by itself, does not directly predict the probability of default. Scores are calibrated, using real-world data, to show so-called 'bad odds' rates. 'Bad odds' are basically the observed default rates within groups of borrowers with the same credit score. Individual defaults are, of course, binary people either default or they do not. Credit scores cannot predict individual defaults, but they can position individuals among pools of people where the pool can be expected to exhibit a measurable default rate.

ALTERNATIVE DATA TO THE RESCUE?

Since the passing of the Fair Credit Reporting Act in 1970, Bureau data have been transformative in enabling widespread lending that is reliable and fair. These data have been essential for generating the $12.3 trillion in outstanding consumer debt in the U.S.

Over the last several years, however, industry participants have searched for additional reliable data sources that can provide information on a consumer's ability to honour financial commitments.

Alternative data may provide additional financial payment information on consumers or otherwise provide information with predictive power; some of the sources of such data are:

- Utilities (gas, water, electricity)
- Telecom (TV, mobile, broadband)
- Rent
- Property/asset record: including value of owned assets.
- Public records: beyond the limited public records information already found in standard credit reports
- Alternative lending payments (e.g., payday, instalment loan, rent-to-own, buy-here-pay-here auto loans, auto title loans): including both on-time and derogatory payment data.
- Demand deposit account (DDA) information: including recurring payroll deposits and payments, average balance, etc.

Several of these alternative data sources involve records of whether a consumer makes payments that they have committed to making (rent, utilities). In credit bureau jargon, when someone fails to make such payments and that is reported to a bureau it is referred to as 'negative data'; conversely, when on-time payments are reported to a bureau it is referred to as 'positive data'. The traditional credit bureau market in the US is based on both types of data, but mostly just for payments made on loans. If alternative data were also to be reported, there is some debate about whether positive, or negative, or both types of data should be reported. This is a point we will return to later. The value of alternative data varies by source. Data like rent payments have been shown to be predictive and may be available for many consumers with no credit file (although many landlords now demand credit scores for new tenants!), But the rental market is very fragmented and data are not uniformly reported. Therefore, coverage is low. Public records data are available on even more people than those with files at the credit bureaus, so their coverage is very wide. However, since the information contained in public records is not explicitly focused on payments, it is not as predictive as credit bureau data; nevertheless, it also proves to be additive in scores developed from combined data sources. The main characteristics of a good source of alternative data are these:

Coverage: a new data source will ideally have broad and consistent coverage (e.g., over 90% of U.S. adults use a cell phone, and the market is concentrated so data collection would be easy to achieve; approximately 40% of U.S. adults pay rent, but this is a low concentration market, and so the data are expensive to collect).

Specificity: a data source should ideally contain detailed data elements about an individual—data elements that provide part of a full picture of the borrower (e.g., on-time and late payments over a significant time series, or specific asset or income data); some data sources are based on 'segment data' or 'modelled data' and are typically less predictive than consumer-specific sources.

Accuracy and timeliness: data should be accurate and frequently updated; a data source should have a system for ongoing data verification and management.

Predictive power ('signal'): most important, data should contain information relevant to the behaviour that you're trying to predict.

Orthogonality: Ideally, the data source should be additive to traditional bureau data; this means that using it will improve the predictive accuracy of any new score by improving the signal-to-noise ratio

Regulatory compliance: data sources must comply with existing regulations for consumer credit (i.e., Fair Credit Reporting Act, Equal Credit Opportunity Act, Gramm-Leach- Bliley Act).

One important development of the last few years has been the realization by big banks that internal data is also 'alternative data' and can play a role in predicting default behaviour. Checking account data, in particular, has been shown to predict repayment behaviour and to enhance the predictive power of traditional credit scores. This seems so intuitively obvious that it is surprising the idea took so long to emerge. But patterns of transaction and balance behaviour in consumer and small business checking accounts can be used to predict default behaviour quite well, and to enhance the predictive power of established credit scores. We are aware of a few banks that have developed and deployed such enhancements or who are in the process of doing so—indeed some of them

183

are our clients. We expect this to become the norm over the next 5–10 years. There is even a possibility that consumer and small business checking account data could become available to third-parties and not just to the banks who manage the accounts. If the US adopts its own equivalent of the EU's Payment Services Directive and related 'Open API' movement, then it could lead to the availability of such data in enhanced credit score development. These moves would empower consumers to make their data available to credit grantors, via data intermediaries (who could be the existing credit bureaus or new players) but only with the permission of the consumer.

We also expect the availability of third-party alternative data to broaden and deepen, possibly even through legislative initiatives to require reporting to the established bureaus.

There have been periodic moves in the US towards mandating the reporting of some alternative data to the credit bureaus.

BENEFITS OF ALTERNATIVE DATA

Having more data is only valuable if it results in real incremental benefits; in this case, the benefits of using alternative data in addition to traditional Bureau data, beyond just technical improvements to the credit score, should flow to both consumers and lenders.

As discussed earlier, many newly scoreable consumers should ideally now be part of a sufficiently accurate risk-separation pattern that a fraction of them also become lendable.

That is, they have to have a score above the cut-offs used by most lenders.

For consumers, the use of alternative data provides two distinct benefits: first, more potential borrowers will be able to secure a loan, including many from among today's credit invisibles. In a recent Experian study where energy utility trade line data were added to the file, almost half of the subprime participants moved up to either the nonprime or prime category.

Second, most existing borrowers will have access to lower interest rates; that is, they will receive more favorable pricing because the small percentage of bad risks will be better separated from the good risks than is possible with traditional scores.

The same Experian study showed that even for customers that remain in a given risk segment (subprime, nonprime, prime), moving from thin-file to full-file yields some improvement in pricing.

As an example, the average credit card interest rate fell from 23% to 21%, a 10 percent reduction, for those (previously thin-file) subprime borrowers who had sufficient utility payment history to qualify them as full-file7. This is an important and often-overlooked benefit in the push to add alternative data.

As we have seen, the objective of a credit score is to separate likely good borrowers from likely bad ones; effective sources of alternative data must, therefore, provide a finer separation within and across credit score bands, improving the accuracy of credit scores. In other words, better credit scores will be better precisely because they can cluster bad in greater concentration at the low-score end of the spectrum. This means that the combination of alternative data and traditional Bureau data should improve the score-versus- bad-odds relationship for the new score such that there will be an observable decrease in default rates associated with higher and mid-level credit score bands and an observable increase in associated default rates in lower credit score bands. In other words, 'the curve will become steeper'. Exhibit 5 illustrates the effect of adding new data that improve the accuracy of existing scores and allow credit invisibles to be meaningfully scored.

For lenders, the primary benefit of alternative data is the increased number of profitable loans to be made consistent with a given risk appetite. Additional benefits may include reduced transaction costs (additional borrower information could reduce the need for manual processes) and lower aggregate credit losses for any cut-off defined by a marginal loss rate.

Also, by having a complete picture of prospective borrowers, lenders will be better positioned to offer competitive interest rates, which many lenders cite as a challenge today.

Some people have expressed concern that alternative data could further marginalize vulnerable credit-excluded populations. They argue that alternative data reporting should include only positive data (meaning on-time payments) and not negative data (payments made late). This may seem humane in that it targets the inclusion of data on deserving people, while discreetly ignoring late-payers, but it doesn't actually help the late-payers even as it subtly undermines the overall ability to provide accurate scores and default probabilities on timely payers. Besides, if a landlord was only reporting a renter's timely payments and then suddenly one month filed no report. To the extent that is not actually true (the renter may have moved out), it would be better simply to report all payments, timely or not. It certainly would support more accurate risk assessment across the entire population. This is an area where many policy proposals to date have been less-than-entirely logical.

New Credit Score Systems Could Open Lending to More Consumers

THE credit reporting industry is starting to unveil alternative credit scores that use more than just bank and credit card information and allow lenders to extend credit to more consumers.

Fair Isaac, the creator of the widely used FICO credit score, has been testing a new score with major credit card lenders for the last year that makes use of alternative data, like cable and cell phone bills, to help assess the likelihood that a borrower will repay a loan.

Now the TransUnion, one of the three major credit reporting bureaus, is introducing its own alternative system, aimed at assigning scores to people who may have low traditional scores or lack them entirely.

TransUnion said on Thursday that its new scoring system combined alternative data with a more nuanced analysis of typical credit data. Called Credit Vision Link, the system allows lenders to assign scores to 95 percent of American adults, said Mike Mondelli, TransUnion's senior vice president of alternative data services.

The alternative models are emerging even as information about traditional credit scores is more widely available to consumers. The new scores use different types of information, as well as new ways of analyzing traditional credit data, to assess the creditworthiness of consumers who have had difficulty borrowing money. About 26 million Americans, or 11 percent of the adult population, lack credit files and are "credit invisible," while 8 percent have some history but not enough to generate a score, the Consumer Financial Protection Bureau says.

Traditional credit scores are based on information reported by banks and credit card companies to the major credit bureaus. But, in what is often a frustrating Catch-22, many consumers can't qualify for loans, or they may have stopped using credit after suffering a financial crisis, so they don't have a financial footprint to create a score. Lenders are reluctant to do business with such consumers because they are unsure whether the borrowers are likely to pay back a loan.

The new methods assign scores to those consumers using different measures. FICO's new score, FICO Score

XD, was developed by the credit bureau Equifax, which provides data on a cell phone and cable accounts for the score, and LexisNexis Risk Solutions, which provides property records and other public data.

In testing, FICO XD allowed more than half of credit card applicants who were previously unscorable to receive a score, said Jim Wehmann, executive vice president for scores at FICO. "It's definitely an on-ramp," he said.

TransUnion said its new score combined a closer analysis of a consumer's traditional payment history with alternative data for a more precise assessment of risk. For instance, while a traditional score notes whether you make the minimum required credit card payments on time, the new score looks at the size of your monthly payment, and whether payments are increasing or decreasing over time, Mr Mondelli said.

In addition, the new score considers factors like how often a consumer changes his or her home address, data from payday loans, as well checking account history, like whether accounts were closed for bounced checks.

The Credit Vision Link score is meant to supplement traditional credit bureau information, Mr Mondelli said. In some instances, he said, the added data may cause a consumer's risk profile to worsen, but most of the time it helps. In tests with a major auto lender, TransUnion said, the new score resulted in up to 24 percent more loan approvals.

While the new methods could potentially help underserved consumers gain access to credit, they could also hurt some people, depending on what information is used and how it is applied, said Chi Chi Wu, a lawyer with the National Consumer Law Center.

"With alternative scoring, the devil is in the details," she said. "It really depends on the type of alternative data and how it's being used.

For instance, it is not clear how accurate telecommunications account data is overall. And subprime loans, like payday loans, currently are not reported to credit bureaus, so adding them to the mix could also harm a consumer's credit report, she said.

Here are some questions and answers about alternative credit scoring:

- Are the new scoring systems currently being used by lenders?
- FICO's new score is in a test phase with a dozen big credit card lenders and is expected to be more broadly available early next year. TransUnion said its new scoring system would be used by several lenders by the end of this year. Neither company would identify its participating lenders.
- What range do the alternative scores use?

- Like traditional credit scores, the alternative scores use a three-digit number, and the higher the score, the lower the risk to the lender. Both FICO XD and TransUnion's Credit Vision Link scores range from 300 to 850.
- Will I be able to get a copy of the report used to generate alternative scores?
  Consumers may obtain a free copy of their credit report once a year from each of the three major

credit bureaus (The TransUnion, Equifax and Experian), at annualcreditreport.com. If consumers are scored using Credit Vision Link, the alternative data will become part of their TransUnion credit report, the company said.

With FICO XD, consumers will be able to obtain a free copy of their report from Equifax and LexisNexis. However, she noted that the scores are not yet generally available. FICO had not yet decided whether to include FICO XD scores in FICO's "open access" program, in which lenders give consumers their credit score free of charge.

ALTERNATIVE CONSUMER REPORTS

Detail these alternative consumer reports

Alternative data

Opportunity facts refer to bills reporting financial records contained in a credit report, consisting of the verbal exchange, charge for strength.

Types of Alternative Data

Alternative data in detailed financial data refers to can be used to evaluate credit chance. This information includes:

Water money owed (e.g., Power, fuel, heating oil)

Invoice telecommunications (e.g., cell telephone)

Lease price, digital payment (financial institution transfer, classification, transfers,

The Opt-Out List

https://www.stopdatamining.me/opt-out-list/

StopDataMining.me Is a central Web portal for critical facts.

(1) consumers perceive themselves and how they acquire and use the customer data and

(2) details of an entrance to receive rights to other selections they offer with appreciate the patronage they hold.

Statistics middleman pioneer and advanced generation to acquire data on consumer conduct offline, online and mobile. But they are slowly developing modern ways for purchasers to get this information for marketing functions, use, proportion, and sell. Now, federal regulators are forcing information brokers to do greater transparent paintings.

In 2012, the federal trade commission turned into suggested to document that the enterprise had mounted a public get right of entry to the internet site to display your name, touch data and data suppliers within the United States tax revenue, and use facts to explain customer rights and greater. Throughout the 12 months, but, there was also a rush to create a centralized portal for customers

The alternative free report "Federal agents: name for transparency and responsibility" that information companies collect, broker of record factors by covering almost all the U.S. billions. As an instance, data broker Acxiom, unmarried, holds additional facts from the client transactions 1.4 billion and 700 billion, statistics features. Also, Acxiom provides more than 3 billion places new records to its database every month.

"The scope of these customer profiles real estate facts days method regularly identifies more us than the circle of friends of relatives, friends, and online shopping in our secular, political affiliations, spaces, and socioeconomic and other activities.

"It's the right time to provide transparency, the judges and the obligation to carry on this industry on behalf of clients, many of whom are unaware that data exists for records" agents offer today pick customers their information, alternatives are widely an incomplete.

As we all know that the secret to our private statistics is very vital and valuable business entrepreneurs — and to accumulate and is offered with the help of many data brokers. Stop datamining. I list hyperlink's joining to prevent those traders' brokers aggregation information about stats on the line is disconnected or sports information.

An important source for the buyer is another way to draw their votes, roughly how to analyze whether the data broker has the type of data available

How to opt out from ACXION

Acxiom

In online Opt-Out, select the easiest-to-use query procedure to get the data. An inability or a substantial value, to get information about you from Acxiom in the United States through marketing can have two results:

Reduce the amount of spam you receive from groups you do and

couples to minimize the relevance of promotional activities you will get from the organization you are experiencing, also, Acxiom customers. Learn more about https://isapps.acxiom.com/optout/optout.aspx

Equifax Inc.

One of the three primary lending reporting companies

Equifax changed into putting in as a retail lending enterprise in Atlanta, Georgia and 1899. The agency grew swiftly and had places to work in 1920 on U.S. And Canada. With the decade of 1960, the retail lending commercial enterprise organization became one of the essential credit score bureaus inside the united states of America of us to preserve files of hundreds of thousands of Americans and Canada residents. Despite the fact that they have been nevertheless reporting the majority of the credit rating, their enterprise was sporting out reviews on coverage organizations even as human beings achieved for brand new insurance policies which include existence, vehicles, fireplace and medical insurance.

All essential coverage corporations use RCC to get facts on health, customs, ethics, vehicle and monetary utilization. He moreover insisted on insurance and suggested employment while humans had been in search of the latest task. Maximum of the credit score work became backed with the aid of business dealers, shops.

Equifax facts services LLC keeps credit files and offers records to some clients, together with credit score card agencies and lenders, to imparting pre-Authorized customers as allowed in **FCRA**.

Equifax, in particular in the company, operates a related evaluation for trading inside the industrial corporation location, a series of patron loans and coverage critiques and sales industries, commercial agency clients embody stores, coverage groups, fitness provider groups, utilities, authority's organizations, banks, credit unions, individuals and specialized financial institutions, and different financial corporations. Equifax enterprise sells credit rating critiques, analysis, demographic facts, and software program. The credit document offers precise data on personal loans and shows that the personal fee information respects the economic duties as to the way to pay the bills or pay off the loan. The credit provides this fact to determine the type and situations of the service or product which you provide. Equifax additionally gives a commercial credit score document just like black & blood, which encompass financial and non-monetary statistics on all scale industrial business enterprise. Equifax collects and offers records via non-credit rating information currencies, which include facts of patron charge of software bills.

Equifax credit score client area added to offer offerings which encompass credit rating fraud and identity theft merchandise from 1999

Before deciding to opt out:

Pre-screened offers can provide many benefits, mainly if you are within the marketplace for a credit card or insurance. Pre-screened can be more favorable than the ones which are available to most of the people. Some credit score card or coverage merchandise can also simplest be to be had via pre screened gives, and because you are pre-selected to acquire the offer, you can only be turned down in confined situations.

All the main insurance organizations use RCC to get statistics on fitness, customs, ethics, car and financial usage. He additionally insisted on coverage and reported employment while people had been in search of a brand-new task. Most of the credit work became subsidized using commercial dealers, shops.

Equifax, specifically in the enterprise, operates an associated evaluation for trading in the commercial enterprise area, a sequence of customer loans and insurance reviews and sales industries, commercial enterprise clients encompass retailers, insurance organizations, health service companies, utilities, authorities businesses, banks, credit unions, individuals and specialized monetary establishments, and other financial firms. Equifax enterprise sells credit score reviews, analysis, demographic data, and software program. The credit report gives accurate information on non-public loans and suggests that the personal charge records respect the financial responsibilities as to the way to pay the bills or repay the loan. The credit provides use of this records to decide the sort and conditions of the product or service which you offer. Equifax additionally offers a commercial credit score record similar to black & blood, which include economic and non-financial information on all scale commercial enterprise. Equifax collects and provides information through non-credit score information currencies, telephone businesses, and records of purchase payment of utility bills.

Equifax credit consumer region added to provide services which include credit score fraud and identification theft merchandise from 1999. To know more of this company. https://help.equifax.com/app/answers/detail/a_id/2/noIntercept/1/kw/prescreen

Experian

One of the three biggest credit reporting groups in the America. Experian offers quite a number services to customers and businesses through its online machine. The primary attention of the business enterprise's work is to provide clients with the essential equipment to maintain and enhance their credibility to be able to ensure their financial freedom. The use of enterprise offerings affords the business enterprise with getting entry to customer credit documents.

As with other foremost credit reporting stations, Experian is widely regulated by way of the appropriate credit score reporting act (FCRA) with the aid of America. 2003 proper and correct credit buying and selling laws signed on 2003 laws, and credit score report agencies want to regulate FCRA to offer purchasers with a loose replica in their credit reports for a 12-month duration. Like it's important competition, TransUnion, and Equifax, Experian market credit reviews immediately to clients. Profit for the Experian marketplace is closely attractive to credit score reporting service, and credit score reviews for all three establishments that may be criticized and brought even to get for free of charge.

Choose-out of pre-accepted proposals

You can cast off your call from a mailing listing supplying credit score or coverage on the Experian display. Visit it site http://www.experian.com/privacy/opting_out_preapproved_offers.html

Your name and statistics (title, email and phone range (profit, collects personal information from applications, surveys and other forms that represent us, including activities, social Security numbers, organization invitations, local restrictions, and industries. We get a record of your work, for example, of our business and interactions.

MYFICO

This company might also acquire non-public information as essential for the supply of services furnished to our clients. However, we may additionally access public resources together with census information, real property statistics private information assets, and marketplace studies information. Observe: an outside carrier provider for a web site can be hosted on a server that is America.

When you visit a website, we may also acquire and save the sender's IP address immediately or via a 3rd birthday party tracking gadget. You can also accumulate aggregated key phrases from your search engine referrals to decide what records your traffic is attempting to find after they look for your website. We do now not permit other events to acquire statistics approximately your online sports from specific websites while you operate the website online or our offerings.

The personal facts you gather may be required for the performance of the services and capabilities supplied through the site. Information collected via web-based tools by collecting statistical data on how to use the website, we will manage and improve our website and user revel in, diagnosing technical troubles occur on our servers.

Perceive individual users who are registered with a particular product and music their sports online, such as their registrations, statements, and requests for data underneath applicable regulation.

Select opt out

For private records, we can no longer take delivery of digital signal tracking reports sent using the browser when we go to different mechanisms which could make alternatives concerning the gathering of our websites or personal information. In addition to 0.33-celebration web sites for online sports over time, you may have the capability to enroll in certain kinds of information and communique to proportion. Tell me why you do no longer:

We may additionally expose statistics about you outside of our corporate organization, but we may divulge records this is required or authorized by law. The vital statistics could be carried out outside of the auditors and the bank government. Allowed revelations, for instance, provide and market us to open, preserve or service your account. (CA, ND, and VT resident: we do no longer divulge data about you out of doors our corporate group inside the organization as required by law or granted if we do now not let you do so.

We will reveal your credit score statistics (financial records from the credit score bureau or assist you to decide your credit score eligibility) within the institution. We do not disclose credit score information outdoor the institution. (VT resident: we do now not reveal any credit information approximately you within our company organization as required using law or granted if we do not let you accomplish that.

To solicit yourself with the aid of electronic mail, telephone or e mail for products or services that aren't without delay related to your account, they're our regular communications with you (e.g., month-to-month statements, customer support email or provider middle when you call our clients). If you do now not solicit yourself, we will not disclose your information within the institution. You MYFICO or free your fico using following the instructions within the media selector software that you can pick out at any time by using logging into your account in www.Myfico.Com while you make a scoring account you can choose to prevent receiving those messages and statistics to cancel the plan, click to your alternatives. In case you get hold of an email from us, you could also forestall emails using the hyperlink subsequent. (Nevada residents: you could also sue the authorities of a hundred Carson St Carson town, NV-89701-4717 or 775-684-1100.

Personal facts, safety, and confidentiality

Updated the physical security measures, including secure regions within the constructing. Digital security measures, together with passwords, can be encrypted both internally and externally. System-kind protection for client approval to prevent identification robbery. The information you provide while you join up for their online product.   For   further   information   visit http://www.myfico.com/policy/privacy-policy/

Freeze SageStream (formerly ID Analytics)

What is SageStream?

SageStream, LLC Credit score reports client reviews agency regulated with the aid of the truthful credit score reporting act (fcra). Sagestream provides information on particular kinds of agencies, along with credit card issuers, shops, wi-fi cell phone provider companies.

For extra facts about your wishes. Visit the legit web site to retrieve their e mail address or fax quantity to send a licensed letter or fax requesting h. Ida to be frozen. Make certain to consist of the following statistics:

The primary call and family

Social security variety

Date of birth

The main telephone wide variety

Deal with including postcode

Two of the following forms of identification:

A duplicate of a driving force's license or state identification card issued by using the country.

"current" cable, software or phone deal with, which corresponds to a replica of the utility to the address indicated in step 1. "lately" is defined as 60 days, that's older than the date of the east, inc., the receipt of the written request to the SSN-a copy of the card.

A copy of an SSN card.

A copy of a birth certificate.

A copy of a U.S. passport (picture page only).

A copy of a voided consumer check with an address matching the address you provided in Step 1.

A copy of an Alien Registration Card.

For those living in Pennsylvania, it's not possible to fax in your request for this report to be frozen.

Consumer Report by SageStream

It's always a good practice to obtain a copy of your consumer report, also referred to as a "credit report" or a "disclosure report," to know what information is being reported about you and to ensure that the information is accurate. If you believe that information contained in your report is not accurate, you can take steps to dispute it. As a general matter, requesting a copy of your consumer report does not adversely affect your credit score since it is not considered to be a "hard" inquiry that a potential creditor would make when you apply for credit or open an account.

Information:

Your first name, middle name, last name, suffix (if applicable)

Your current address including ZIP code

Your current phone number with area code

Your Social Security numbers

Your date of birth (month, day, and year)

For security purposes, we must verify your identity. Therefore, please include the following with your written request:

A legible copy of your current driver's license or other current government-issued identification card showing your current address and date of birth.

If the ID that issued your driver's license or other government doesn't, or if he does not show the current shipping address, readable copy of a document required from the range listed below.

If you don't have a driver's license or ID card issued by another Government, legible copy of a document from category 1 and two categories listed below are required.

Category 1

Social Security card

U.S. passport picture page

Alien registration card

Military identification card (front and back)

Category 2

Recent cable, utility or telephone statement with your name and current mailing address. `

Bank statement with current address

Rental lease agreement showing current address

Voided personal check with your preprinted current address

Notarized letter from your landlord confirming your current name and residential address

Mortgage statement with the current address

File Dispute

SageStream requires that you have a copy of your SageStream consumer report before filing a dispute If you do not have one, the first step in submitting a dispute is to obtain a copy of your Sagestream consumer report, which will contain your information. Instructions on how to get a copy of your consumer report can be found on the user. Once you have reviewed your report, specify the information they share, and state that you will return the report to us, explaining why you think the information is inaccurate, incomplete, or not of your own.

When they have been disputed, they explore the sources of information available to them through contact. The results of the survey will be sent if the exact source in your portfolio is dark verified. To upgrade these conflicts, you must work directly with the source.

The axis of the dispute is determined by the Fair Credit Reporting Act, and in most cases, the investigation must be completed within 30 days of your dispute. If the information you provide confirms this contention, the time required to complete will be extended to 15 days.

Secured fax:

(858) 312-6275

Or

Postal mail:

SageStream, LLC Consumer Office

P. O. Box 503793

San Diego, CA 92150

How to request a copy of your consumer report

Blocking Information as a Result of Identity Theft

If you suppose that your patron record came about as a result of identity robbery, you may request information about fraud be blocked from your record. Blocking off facts will prevent your credit score file or Sagestream of those companies, which have the criminal proper to gain it. However, it does not encompass accurate records you watched is related to identity theft. In most cases, it is recommended that you first obtain a copy of your consumer report from SageStream to review the information we Now you have got on. Instructions on the way to acquire a copy of your patron record can be located on the consumer reviews.

To request particular statistics approximately the identification robbery consumer record, you can apply for a replica of the file to specify the facts you need to dam fraud; you may need to offer us with the model id robbery file of Chen. For records approximately, the way to create one with the federal alternate fee (FTC) and reviews of identity theft, see the FTC at www.consumer.ftc.gov. Send your request and copy of your Identity

Theft Report to us at:

Secured fax:

(858) 312-6275

Or

Postal mail:

SageStream, LLC Consumer Office

P. O. Box 503793

San Diego, CA 92150

Opt-Out / Opt-In from the credit agents

If you do not want to get undesirable presets or provide earlier popularity of the credit factors and insurance of the business, they may be positioned out with assistance in making use of for "return" from mailing lists. Your choice to withdraw from receiving these offers for five years or wholly.

If you do not want unwanted or pre-permitted pre-credit factors and coverage of organizations, you could get out of mailing listing together with your request can be processed inside five operating days of receipt. You'll discover a maintain of a confirmation letter that includes a ramification of personal identification (pins) continues to use stream inside the future, in case you get a pre-approval of credit points and insurance for "constant in," and you're required to offer a pin will determine.

If you have previously selected and determine that you want to get hold of a pre-approval credit score rating and coverage from groups that permit your credit of the reporting amount, you will be required to "determine" by using finishing the choice as polls, dispatched to the fountain in fax wide variety a. And cope with cited above.

216

First call, middle name, final name, suffix (if applicable)

Contemporary consists of dealing with that zip

Modern phone with extensive variety site code

Social security wide variety

Start date (month, date, year)

In case your request is to be separated with five years, completely or with assistance that decides to apply to "decide-out." You have five years or usually the choice to withdraw from receiving these presents for a period. Check for extra records and new update of the site https://www.sagestreamllc.com/opt-out-opt-in/

2. ARS (Advanced Resolution Services)

ARS is a subsidiary of Visa, and they don't have a dedicated website (which is really in violation of the **FCRA** as contact information is supposed to be displayed and available to the general public).

ARS doesn't have a website but here is their contact information: 5005 Rockside Road, Suite 600

Independence, OH 44131 or fax: 216-615-7642

Send a certified letter or fax asking for your credit report to be frozen Include all of the following information

First and last name

Social security number

Full address

Primary contact number

Your signature

Two forms of identification:

A copy of a state-issued driver's license or state identification card.

A copy of a U.S. passport (picture page only)

A copy of an SSN card

A copy of a birth certificate

A copy of an Alien Registration Card

Sample Letter

Advanced Resolution Service, INC (Company Name)

5005 Rockside Road, Suite 600 (Street Address)

Independence, OH 44131 ((City, State, Postcode)

To Whom It May Concern

I am writing to you to put a security freeze on my credit report. Under the Fair Credit Report Act, you're required to comply. My information is clearly shown below:

Full Name: (First Name), (Last Name)

Social Security Number: (SSN)

Current Address: (Current Address)

Previous Address: (Only Include If You Moved in The Last 2 Years>

Primary Contact Number: (Primary Contact Number)

I've included the following two documents that verify my identity:

(Name of document one)

(Name of document two)

After this credit freeze has been filed, can you also please send me written confirmation to the address listed above.

Kind regards,

(First Name), (Last Name)

(Signature)

(Date signed)

Final Word

In case you are interested to see what's virtually on your credit score report from each of these credit score reporting corporations, you furthermore might have the right to see a replica once consistent with yr. You shouldn't have any problem inquiring for this along with your credit freeze. Ensure you follow all of those steps before applying for any united states of America bank card

What is ARS? (advance resolution service)

ARS is a bureau that keeps track of how many cards have been applied for from your address, in addition to other stuff - but that's the main thing that people get dinged for.

Using my magic ESP powers, did you recently apply for a credit card and get rejected? If so, it's likely ARS suggesting you get a copy of your report and make sure that it is valid so that you may be approved in the future if there are mistakes on it.

1. ChexSystems

Chex Systems, Inc. (ChexSystems) is a nationwide specialty consumer reporting agency under the federal Fair Credit Reporting Act (FCRA). ChexSystems' clients regularly contribute information on closed checking and savings accounts.

ChexSystems Consumer Score

Correct credit report Federal Act (**FCRA**) promotes the accuracy, equity, and the list of documents for the information report. There are many types of clients saying to businesses, including the corporate Bureau credit score point (including promoting corporate facts, history writing in the condominium register diagnostic information and facts).

Considered one of the FCRA rights below to request your credit rating. The legal credit score based on your total listings-credit eligibility numbers mainly credit Bureau. You can ask the credit rating business reporting consumer ratings or distribute the person's rank or by arranging the loan, but you can pay or accept it. Some loans transactions, you will receive credit score information for free from the mortgage lender.

Request Your ChexSystems Consumer Score

The ChexSystems Consumer Score and scoring model may be different than the credit score used by a recipient of your consumer report. Because a credit score is merely a snapshot of a consumer report at the time the score was calculated, the score will change to reflect changes in the report. There are a wide variety of credit scores available, and each creditor may use a different score or may give more or less weight to the score they use in relation to other factors. ChexSystems Consumer Scores range from 100 to 899, with a higher score indicating a lower risk

You can request Your for ChexSystems Consumer Score by

Mail

Chex Systems, Inc.

Attention: Consumer Relations

7805 Hudson Road, Suite 100

Woodbury, MN 55125

Fax

602.659.2197

Requesting a ChexSystems Consumer Score for a Minor

You must be 18 years of age or older to request your ChexSystems Consumer Score. If you are requesting a Consumer Score on behalf of a minor, you must submit your request by mail and include the following information:

A notarized copy of the minor's birth certificate

A legible copy of the minor's Social Security card

A legible copy of the parent or guardian's driver's license or state identification card

Proof of address for the parent or guardian (in the form of a pay stub, utility bill or other official document bearing the address to which correspondence is to be sent).

If your name does not appear on the birth certificate, a copy of a document confirming legal guardianship is required. This proof of guardianship must be an official court or another legally binding document.

Once your request has been received, ChexSystems will send a response to you via U.S. mail within fifteen business days.

For more information on scores, you may view the answers to the for more information on scores, most frequently asked questions.

Here are some of FAQ's you can see on the site

a. Why did my ChexSystems consumer report receive the score it did?

Your ChexSystems Consumer Score is based on information contained in your consumer file. By reviewing the key factors that impact your score, you can gain a better understanding of your score.

b. Why do companies I want to do business with use scores?

Potential lenders or other creditors want to see how you have fulfilled your past credit obligations to assist them in determining if they are able to approve your request for credit with them and to help them determine the terms of that credit.

c. **How can I manage or improve my score?**

Scores can change gradually over time as your overall credit and debit history changes. There is no quick remedy for eliminating past credit history that may be affecting your score. There are many credit repair companies doing business today, but you should be very cautious and avoid any companies that offer to remove late payments or other accurate information from your credit history. It is illegal for these companies to offer to remove accurate and timely negative items from your credit history. If you are unsure about a company's credibility, you should contact the Better Business Bureau before doing business with them. The best approach for managing your score is to manage your credit and debit activities responsibly over time. You should review the key factors provided with your score. These are the main elements or factors affecting your score.

e. **Do all ChexSystems customers receive the same score?**

Not Every client of ChexSystems services may consider a range of factors (together with your ChexSystems client rating) and hire its hazard control techniques in connection with its selections whether to approve a software and on what terms. The ChexSystems customer score and scoring model can be distinctive than the credit score utilized by a recipient of your customer document. Because a credit score rating is simply a picture of a client file at the time the rating became calculated, the rating will alternate to mirror adjustments inside the file. There is a wide sort of credit ratings to be had and each lender can also use an extraordinary score, or may additionally deliver more or less weight to the score they use with regards to other elements.

d. What are ChexSystems Consumer Score ranges?

ChexSystems Consumer Scores range from 100 to 899, with a higher score indicating a lower risk.

Identity Theft Information

What to do if your identity has been stolen

In this situation, you are to contact the fraud departments of the three major credit bureaus listed below for immediate action.

Verification Services Equifax

Equifax Verification Services:

The paintings variety offers a couple one of a kind services that make life less complicated at work. If your company uses the w-2 service from Equifax personnel solutions, you'll be capable of getting entry to your w-2s through the work wide variety account.

W-2 service offers a fast and efficient way to get copies of your W-2, and even down load it directly into your tax go back. No extra looking forward to it to arrive using email, now not to mention you dispose of the threat of it getting lost. By the way, if you find a mistake on your w-2, your company may additionally even provide you the option to request a correction thru our provider.

As with every offering provided thru the paintings number, our w-2 provider is comfortable. Only you've got access to your account, and all transactions are encrypted to   protect   your

privacy similarly. https://www.theworknumber.com/employe
es/W2/

To order your report, call: 800.685.1111 or write:

Disclosure Info, PO Box 105851, Atlanta, GA 30348

To report fraud, call: 800.525.6285 or write:

Fraud Info, PO Box 105069, Atlanta, GA 30348

Hearing impaired call 800.255.0056 and ask the operator to call the Auto Disclosure Line at 800.685.1111 to request a copy of your report.

Experian - http://www.experian.com/

The result is only money is advanced through the payment system is clear, direct and comprehensive investment facts, which emphasizes unparalleled accuracy and precision.

This funding. The opportunity to leverage the demographic forecast of Experian Marketing strategies and proprietary advanced analytics to provide home financing, "including an estimate for the U.S. 's 110 million

The score allows for information analysis, strategic planning and marketing experts and sales expansion strategies and processes across the full life cycle, from the possibility of purchase-save.

Unmatched statistics basis

Not like different answers that depend upon stale, self-stated information situation to sampling errors and response bias, wealth possibility rating is the only wealth-estimation model developed the use of demonstrated and direct-measured investor facts, mentioned monthly by way of extra than 800 financial circumstances participants.

Wealth opportunity rating changed into created and is run with the aid of Experian, the global chief for consumer records management, offering professional insights, analytical gear, and marketing offerings to companies and purchasers. The rating turned into evolved using direct-measured investor statistics from broad ridge financial solutions, the primary provider of proxy vote casting services for extra than 90 percent of banks, broker-dealers, mutual budget, coverage agencies and publicly traded groups within the united states of America, supplying unequaled competitive profits.

Unparalleled facts granularity

Whether or not you need to goal families with $one hundred,000, $100 million or $1 billion in investable belongings, wealth opportunity score provides remarkable information granularity — asset degrees begin in thousand-dollar increments without a cap. The score is calibrated monthly to reflect stock marketplace changes, wealth transfers, and family moves, permitting you to measure development in target-advertising projects and become aware of new opportunities with unmatched precision.

Comprehensive coverage of customer wealth

Rating forecast cash leverages Experian's demographic, marketing forecast techniques and proprietary advanced analytics to offer general family finance estimates 110 million American families. The result represented a total investment of liquid funds, including equity, alternative business price limits, budget, debt, mutual funds and cash deposits of cash both held their firm and other companies. This allows you to concentrate on the economic potential of the family with the best precision, to focus resources on houses with the greatest possibility for growth.

Advantage a competitive area

Wealth possibility rating offers you a strategic advantage over the opposition using enabling you to:

Full Client life cycle (acquisition, go boost, sell and retention) is

230

enough to create customized ads to optimize money management, brokerage, insurance, and marketing efforts for retail banking products and that resonates with your audience marketing and Ownership score for the Enterprise-Program stats plan-determine the product approach for expanding my own patron relationship control (CRM) database, customer on board, acquisition, loyalty programs and Account Control for current day pockets and lifetime value Develop part of the measures clients and possibilities

Wealth opportunity score can be introduced in any of the following codecs:

Rating append to customer CRM report

Score attach to customer-furnished prospect listing

Experian-generated prospect listing based on client specifications the direct information feed into any decisions as a services advertising module (e.g., retail financial institution customer move-sell).

learn more http://www.experian.com/consumer-information/wealth-data/wealth-opportunity-score.html

To order your report, call: 888.397.3742 or write:

Disclosure Info, PO Box 2002, Allen, TX 75013

To report fraud, call: 888.397.3742 or write:

Fraud Info, PO Box 9554, Allen, TX 75013

TDD: 800.972.0322

3. **Trans Union**

"TransUnion's alternative data credit score enables Sierra Auto

Finance to assess the creditworthiness of thin-file applicants better. We found that a majority of thin-file applicants have previously used alternative credit products, but a majority of these loans are not reported to traditional credit bureaus. TransUnion brings traditional and alternative credit data together, and that allows us to extend credit responsibly to customers who demonstrate they have the ability to repay the loan. The company analysis revealed a strong correlation between historical alternative loan performance and future auto loan performance. As a result, Sierra's current custom application score is significantly more predictive than our previous custom application score." **Jeremy Jones TransUnion** delivers a 360-degree view of individuals, businesses and vendors with an aggregated, networked view of public and private non-FCRA regulated information:

FCRA alternative data options

Our FCRA-compliant assets include CreditVision® LinkSM, the first score in the market to combine trended and alternative data sources for a more precise look at consumer risk, and DriverRiskSM, which provides unique insight into driver risk with comprehensive court record data.

Non-FCRA opportunity data alternatives

Our clients can explore connections between human beings, groups, belongings, and locations; perceive property, uncover inconsistencies and become aware of misrepresentations; and uncover evidence of economic misery or crook interest. Our merchandise encompasses Tloxp; car records score powered with the aid of Carfax, and commercial habitational answer.

For further information, check here http://www.transunion.com/

To order your report, call: 800.888.4213 or write:

Disclosure Info, PO Box 1000, Chester, PA 19016

To report fraud, call: 800.680.7289 or write:

Fraud Info, PO Box 2000, Chester, PA 19016

TDD: 877.553.7803

Place a security alert on your ChexSystems consumer data

Contact all financial institutions where you have accounts that an identity thief has taken over or created in your name but without your knowledge. Cancel those accounts, place stop-payment orders on any outstanding checks that may not have cleared, and change your Automated Teller Machine (ATM) card, account, and personal identification number.

File a police report and get a copy of the report to be used if need to show proof of the crime

Contact the Federal Trade Commission (FTC) to file a complaint.

Access the FTC's ID Theft website https://www.identitytheft.gov/

Call toll-free at 877.IDTheft (877.438.4338)

TDD at 202.326.2502

Send mail to Consumer Response Center, FTC, 600 Pennsylvania

Avenue, N.W., Washington, DC 20580

You can as well contact the US Postal Inspection Service https://postalinspectors.uspis.gov/ at U.S. Postal Inspector Service or the Social Security Administration at 800.629.0271.

Protect your identity

There are numerous things you can do to reduce the chance that you'll become a victim:

Protect your checkbook and supply of checks.

You should not put bills paid with checks inside your mailbox for postal pickup.

Safe guard your identity. Keep bank account numbers, personal identification numbers (PIN) and Social Security number out of your pocketbook and wallet.

Destroy financial documents such as old bank statements or credit offers that contain account numbers or account information.

Always write checks in permanent ink.

Use caution when providing financial information over the phone or the Internet.

Review your bank statements or returned checks to verify no unauthorized transactions occurred.

If your wallet or checkbook is lost or stolen, act immediately to reduce the potential for damage to your personal funds and financial information.

Common Mistakes you try to Avoid

A You forgot to stop automatic payments from being taken out before you closed your account.

Make sure to pick out all automated bills and near them earlier than closing your account. If no longer, you can get better wages, even after final the account. When paying stop requests, ask your lady friend to ensure how tons time it takes to manner your application. Groups can frequently take weeks to request changes to pay. Among, additional payments could be deducted from your account.

B. You close your checking account by letting it go to a zero balance.

Always contact your financial institution if you wish to close your account. If you have not closed your account, also formally charged after the account expires. Then you will have a negative balance in your account and possibly the over-drafting fee, which you are responsible for paying for your financial institution. C. A check you deposit in your account does not clear or bounces, causing the account to go into overdraft.

Just because you have deposited the check does not guarantee the check has the funds to support it. When depositing checks, allow enough time to make certain the check clears (usually 3-5 days, depending on the institution) before writing checks against the balance.

D. **You wrote a check for more than you have in your account.**

It is very necessary that you balance your checkbook regularly so that you always know your account balance. If you discover that you have written a check for more than you have in your account, instant deposit funds to cover the amount of the check and any associated overdraft fees.

E. **You co-signed on an account that was abused by the other party.**

Very cautious when agreeing with a joint account or becoming a co-signer on someone else's account. Whether the signer has handled the account, both the guarantor can be held responsible

F. You gave your PIN (Personal Identification Number) to someone else, and they took funds from your account without your authorization.

Never give your PIN to someone else. It is like opening the door to your finances. Inform your financial institution of the situation. They may suggest that you change your PIN or they may suggest that you close the compromised account and open a new one.

G. You post-dated a check, and it was cashed too early.

Postdating is a dangerous test because there is no legal obligation to follow on the other party. You should just wait to rely on the other party to check the post-date cash. If the check is cashed, by mistake, you are responsible. Better to wait for the check writer, when you have the money available in your account.

H. You're not receiving statements or correspondence from your financial institution.

If you have moved or changed names, it can sometimes take time for your mailed account statement to catch up with you. Always notify your financial institution when there are changes to your personal information. Not knowing the status of your account does not excuse you from being responsible for it.

I. You discover an account or handling error by the financial institution.

Economic establishments are making errors. Looking at your economic organization reviews and confirmations is crucial. Carry questions or mistakes right now to the monetary institution. Once you do, it's smooth to put on them for economic institutions.

J. Your checks are lost or stolen.

If a check is lost or stolen, report it to your financial institution immediately. Stop paying for the test before they fall into the wrong hands is very easy after someone wrote to check against your account. See counterfeit checks for more information.

TheWorkNumber

TheWorkNumber is a user-paid verification of employment database created by TALX Corporation. TALX was acquired by Equifax Inc. in February 2007.

The number of work permits for asylum seekers to receive immediate confirmation of the person's wages for employment and verification purposes. Payment for this information is only revealed after taking a few questions answered It is used by over 50,000 organizations to verify employment data.

Some organizations that use the Work Number include Fannie Mae, Hilton Hotels, Rent-A- Center, the United States Postal Service,

Domino's Pizza, the University of Pennsylvania, and the University of Missouri System. Founded in 1995, The Work Number has over 225 million employment records.

The Work Number is an example of outsourcing of a Human Resources department function.

Additionally, the adoption of The Work Number causes a change in the financial responsibility for verification of employment. In typical organizations, the cost of a verification of employment is borne completely by the employer, and the actual cost of service is absorbed into the human resource department budget. In organizations using The Work Number, the cost is borne by the requestor of verification, who purchases either a single verification or a package of multiple verifications from TALX.

Data Collected

The Work Number collects week-by-week salary information which is as up to date as the last pay period and can go back many years. They also collect length of employment, job titles, "location information," and "other kinds of human resources-related information, such as health care provider, whether someone has dental insurance and if they've ever filed an unemployment claim

ADVANTAGES:

Cost savings

The service reduces the amount of time required for Human Resource departments to respond to employment verification requests. If Human Resource departments manage a large number of employees, such as universities, seasonal employers, etc. the amount of time savings and cost savings could be considerable.

Access control

Employees of a company or organization using The Work Number's services receive an account that is set up for them on the website. Current, and presumably, former employees can log on to The Work Number at any time.

Employees cannot control access to their records by any entity or person which knows their social security number.

If the employee wishes for a requestor to see his or her salary history, the employee logs on and obtains a 6-digit code, which he or she passes on to the requestor. Without that particular 6-digit code, the requestor is not allowed to view salary of the employee.

Equifax advertises and sells some data to third parties. Companies including "mortgage, auto and other financial services credit grantors" may request pay rate information similar to a credit report. Also, "debt/collection agencies may request employment information" to verify someone's place of employment.

Instant availability of records

Additionally, as soon as the requester receives permission from an applicant to access the record, and the fee is paid (if required), it is instantly available.

Objective nature of records

The system reports factual information only, such as length of employment and job title. Some employers feel this reduces the risk of legal liability over the subjective content of personal references.

Similarly, if an employee is concerned that a supervisor might share unfavorable information or be unwilling to verify employment, The Work Number provides some protection from this, as the system only reports objective data. It does not include performance reviews.

Additional HR services

The WorkNumber, if set up for this service by the employer, may provide duplicate copies of W-2 forms through the employee's online portal.

Social services fee waiver

The WorkNumber generally charges for verification data. However, fees are waived for Federal, State, or County Social Service Departments, who are providing benefits such as the Food Stamp program or TANF to their low-income/welfare applicants. The reports are sent by fax and may take a few days to be sent. Certain expedited services or advanced services may have fees attached.

To qualify for reduced or waived fees, the agency must register with The Work Number using an official fax number. Agencies that can take advantage of this service include eligibility programs, public housing, child support enforcement, and other public assistance needs. A "batch service" for multiple requests is also available.

Criticisms: Privacy Breach

EXCLUSIVE: Your employer may share your salary, and Equifax-owned company called The Work Number might sell that data NBC Red Tape

Equifax Sells Private Information to Debt Collectors In 'Biggest Privacy Breach in Our Time': Report Huffington Post

Security

Recently, internet security issues at sites that contain "sensitive" information has become a big business for hackers. Questions regarding the safety of various websites that offer services (such as The Work Number) that contain this information may be compromised by hackers (and may be a future target for hackers) and a problem for internet security officials. The call center is located in Costa Rica and requires Social Security Number adding more risk to identity theft.

Profit motive

The Work Number charges a fee to the requesting party for each Employment Verification. Requestors can choose a "pay per use" plan or can select a package which includes a certain number of verifications per month.

Because a fee (up to $39.00 per verification) is required, this increases the financial cost of verifying an individual's employment. There is a risk this cost could be passed on to the applicant.

Mandatory usage policies

Some organizations are making use of The Work Number

mandatory as the only way for employees or verifiers to receive information about a staffer's employment. This limits the availability of personalized, subjective, or qualitative references. It also requires a fee be paid each time verification is required.

Inaccurate or out of date information

Some consumers have complained to the Privacy Rights Clearinghouse that "the data in its database is inaccurate," or that "when they try to use the information for employment verification, their titles are outdated or otherwise misrepresent their work history

DATA AGGREGATION

Seven Key Criteria to an Effective Aggregation Solution

Companies today are faced with reporting and data analysis applications that are hamstrung by performance. Market and regulatory pressures are placing company CIOs in difficult positions. Furthermore, the amount of data being collected is increasing as are the demands for more detailed analysis and reporting. Among the areas hardest hit by these challenges are:

The need for timely financial close reporting

Accurate sales and marketing data to develop more profitable customers, and real-time disclosure to meet compliance regulations.

In response, organizations have resorted to all manners of stop-gap measures to coax a performance out of BI applications with little to no success.

What Is Data Aggregation and Why Should You Care?

Data aggregation is any process in which information is expressed in a summary form for purposes such as reporting or analysis. Ineffective data aggregation is currently a major component that limits query performance. And, with up to 90 percent of all reports containing aggregate information, it becomes clear why proactively implementing an aggregation solution can generate significant performance benefits, opening up the opportunity for companies to enhance their organizations' analysis and reporting capabilities.

But how do you go about selecting an effective aggregation solution? First, let's review the typical quick fixes that are used to improve query performance today. Then we'll review the seven key criteria that will help companies evaluate an effective data aggregation solution.

An effective data aggregation solution can be the answer to your query performance problems. Free your organization from the arbitrary restrictions placed on your BI infrastructure as a result of quick fixes, and turn reporting and data analysis applications into strategic, corporate-wide assets.

Don't Settle for Quick Fixes

Traditional approaches to solving ineffective data aggregation are no longer enough

New server hardware. BI applications relying on RDBMS infrastructure perform only incrementally better when additional hardware is introduced. Clearly, the added costs of capital equipment acquisition do not yield the exponential performance improvements required by today's operational BI applications.

Partitioning, de-normalization, and creating derivative data marts and OLAP cubes. Although they are more difficult to implement than many of the other quick fixes, these tried and true techniques have been used for many years to improve query performance. But the reality is that tuning requires time, and is a continuous process that will not improve query performance enough to deliver the timely reports businesses require.

Report caching and broadcasting. While caching may provide some performance relief, global organizations servicing geographically dispersed users find it increasingly difficult to allocate sufficient blocks of time to process these reports. The result of report caching and broadcasting is stale, canned reports that are hours or days old—providing limited benefit in an environment where ad-hoc, on-demand reporting is a requirement.

Summary tables. Anecdotal evidence suggests that organizations build only a limited number of summary tables that cover a very small percentage of all possible user requests. The maintenance burden introduced by even several dozen summary tables quickly outweighs their incremental benefit.

The following key criteria were developed in collaboration with leading BI analysts and practitioners. Companies using these new criteria can now evaluate innovative technologies that have the capability to address ineffective data aggregation.

Seven Key Criteria to Selecting an Effective Aggregation Solution

Enterprise-class solution. Enterprise-class solutions share a number of characteristics that should be required by any company serious about business intelligence.

These solutions are architected to support dynamic business environments. They provide mechanisms to ensure high availability and easy maintenance, they allow for multi- server environments, and they support activities such as backup and recovery. They typically also have more than one way to interface with the system.

Once designed, the solution is easily maintainable; little to no management is necessary.

- The solution must be able to adapt to ever-changing business requirements by having the ability to support changing hierarchies and structures (e.g., attribute to a dimension).
- The system must leverage existing IT investments in BI environments and DB infrastructures.

Integration with the existing applications and systems must be simple. At a minimum, there must be a set of published APIs to popular BI applications and DB systems.

Flexible architecture. A flexible architecture is one that allows for exponential growth and flexibility. This allows the solution provider to be ultra-responsive to the shifting needs of its customers—extremely important, as the business environment is always changing.

- The solution should use standard industry models to support complex aggregation needs.
- The solution should support all types of reports and reporting environments.

The ideal architecture should optimize pre-aggregation with aggregation on the fly.

Performance. Performance refers to the speed, responsiveness, and quality of the application. Queries that take hours to run are no longer acceptable to business users. Moreover, the data they receive must be fresh. The market demands current information in seconds to minutes in order to make judicious business decisions.

- Query performance must be virtually instantaneous.

Users will not be required to trade excessive build (pre-aggregations) times for good query performance.

Performance must be predictable not dependent on users, data, or time-of-day variations.

Scalability. The amount of data being collected is increasing. And, with the proliferation of technologies that facilitate gathering even more transactional data such as RFID, scalability will become even more important to plan for in the future.

- The solution should support billions of rows and tens of dimensions with millions of members. Incremental updates should take minutes per day to enable near- real-time processing.
- The solution should support hundreds to thousands of concurrent users.

Fast implementation. With implementation costs running at two to three times the price of software, it is imperative to evaluate implementation time as well as a product's reliance on expensive IT resources.

- The system should have a proven implementation methodology and approach.
- The GUI tool should provide users with a wizard to speed development.

- The solution should require little to no training.

Utility management and control processes should be in place.

Efficient use of hardware and software resources. Solutions need to be evaluated on their ability to use hardware and software resources efficiently. Systems that promise significant improvements may also require exponentially more resources—which can be unanticipated and costly.

- There should be minimal to no increase in CPU/processing requirements.
- Minimal to no increase in storage requirements (e.g., no more than 20 percent of the storage required to store your fact data).
- The solution should provide embedded compression and caching mechanisms.

Price/performance. The criteria used in selecting the technology requirements must coincide with the value of the solution to make it worth implementing. Making financially responsible decisions is no longer just a goal, but rather a necessity.

- The solution must be priced to scale with the needs of your business.
- There should be no hidden long-term costs associated with supporting the solution.

CONCLUSION

Because consumers cannot see most of the new consumer scores, cannot know the factors underlying many of the scores, there is no real application of Fair Information Principles to many of the new and unregulated consumer scores. Consumers who do not know about the existence or use of the Wealth Score Metric cannot have any say in who used the score, or how. Scores affect the lives of consumers, but only with reform will consumers receive rights to protect their interests.

The alternative data business is changing and is becoming much more sophisticated. Consumer scores are a significant way that this is happening.

Wealth scoring has substantial potential to become a major policy issue as scores with unknown factors and unknown uses and unknown validity and unknown legal constraints move into broader use. Secrecy, the fairness of the factors, the accuracy of the models, and the use of sensitive information is some of the key issues that must be addressed. It is exquisitely unlikely that self-regulation will solve all of the dilemmas wealth scoring introduces. However, we already have at least a partial model for what.